125 best
vegan
recipes

125 best vegan recipes

Maxine Effenson Chuck
& Beth Gurney

Robert
ROSE

For complete cataloguing information, see page 181.

Disclaimer

The recipes in this book have been carefully tested by our kitchen and our tasters. To the best of our knowledge, they are safe and nutritious for ordinary use and users. For those people with food or other allergies, or who have special food requirements or health issues, please read the suggested contents of each recipe carefully and determine whether or not they may create a problem for you. All recipes are used at the risk of the consumer.

We cannot be responsible for any hazards, loss or damage that may occur as a result of any recipe use.

For those with special needs, allergies, requirements or health problems, in the event of any doubt, please contact your medical adviser prior to the use of any recipe.

Design & Production: PageWave Graphics Inc.

Editor: Judith Finlayson

Recipe Editor and Tester: Jennifer MacKenzie

Copy Editor: Christina Anson Mine

Photography: Mark T. Shapiro

Food Styling: Kate Bush

Prop Styling: Charlene Erricson

Cover image: Curried Vegetables with Tofu (page 98)

The publisher and author wish to express their appreciation to the following suppliers of props used in the food photography:

DISHES AND LINENS
Homefront
371 Eglinton Avenue West,
Toronto, Ontario M5N 1A3
Tel: (416) 488-3189
www.homefrontshop.com

DISHES, WOODWARE & LINENS
Caban
396 St. Clair Avenue West,
Toronto, Ontario M5P 3N3
Tel: (416) 654-3316
www.caban.ca

We acknowledge the financial support of the Government of Canada through the Book Publishing Industry Development Program (BPIDP) for our publishing activities.

Published by Robert Rose Inc.
120 Eglinton Avenue East, Suite 800, Toronto, Ontario, Canada M4P 1E2
Tel: (416) 322-6552; Fax: (416) 322-6936

Printed in Canada

2 3 4 5 6 7 8 9 FP 13 12 11 10 09 08 07

From Maxine:

To my incomparable husband, Bill — thank you
for making anything and everything possible.
And to my wonderful girls, Elizabeth and Jennifer —
thank you for inspiring me to always be better.

From Beth:

To my husband, Josh, and daughters,
Oriane, Tatiana and Valentine, and to my parents,
Doris and Clifford Gurney, for their love and support.

Contents

Acknowledgments

THERE WERE SO MANY WONDERFUL PEOPLE who supported us throughout this project, whose contributions we would like to recognize.

From Maxine:

First and foremost, I want to thank my husband, Bill, for encouraging and supporting me, shopping with me, cooking beside me and creating some of the recipes included in this book. Not only is he a masterful home cook, he is also an honest and precise tester. Often he made good recipes significantly better. My children, Elizabeth and Jennifer, were great tasters, who always provided candid and constructive suggestions that resulted in tastier recipes. Elizabeth also tested some recipes and used her considerable writing talents to improve the language in some of the methods. Both girls provided unending encouragement and support throughout the writing process.

Thank you to my family and my many devoted friends, who tirelessly and enthusiastically tested recipes and offered thoughtful and creative feedback. These include: my sister, Andrea Pyenson, without whom this project would not have gotten off the ground, and my mother, Midge Effenson, who contributed some of the original comfort food recipes, which we adapted for the book. In addition, many thanks to my ever-faithful, lifelong camp friends, Sharon Jaffe, Susan Musinsky, Carolyn Randolph, Laurie Samuels (and Amy); extended family members Sharon Morin and Debbie Gammerman; and my friends Nancy Bennett, Warren Clement, Cindy Elcock, Richard Elmore, Esther Kattef, Laura Knott, Bonnie Lass, Jodie Manasevit, Barbara McGinley, and Laura Sproch. I would also like to thank Jack Rossin for contributing two of his delicious, savory recipes to our book.

Finally, I would like to thank Beth for being such a wonderful, inspiring coauthor. Her creativity, expertise, dedication, humor, intelligence, work ethic and upbeat attitude were driving forces that kept this project moving forward.

From Beth:

First and foremost, I want to thank Maxine, my coauthor, for sharing in the delightful process of authorship. Her depth and resourcefulness, as well as her way with words, filled each workday together with joy and learning. She and her husband, Bill, kindly opened the doors to their kitchen, garden and office for this collaboration.

My source, The Farm and Wilderness Camp in Plymouth, Vermont, is a community we cherish. It opened up our family's exposure to nutritious vegan and vegetarian diets. I am thankful for this source of inspiration. Developing recipes to share at home (that passed the teen test) was a fun and adventurous journey, for which I owe a debt of gratitude to my daughters Oriane, Tati and Val, for their helpful feedback. Josh, my husband, offered support every bite of the way and enjoyed making and sharing connections with our work in progress and the world at large. Thank you for all your understanding and support.

My greatest debt of gratitude goes to my mother, Doris Gurney, who offered up her enthusiasm and lifetime experience of large-family cooking to test and refine a number of our recipes. Thanks to my dad, Clifford Gurney, a man of science with a dry sense of humor, who helped with the tasting end of the equation always adding positive energy to advance the process.

My dedicated testers deserve great thanks. They went beyond recipe testing into the science of extra trials and lengthy conversations: Sonja Goldstein, Eunice Ohrt, Rachel Youdelman, Ellen Ogden, Gwen O'Hara, Ellen Forrester, Josie Patterson, Kitty Woods, Anne Sommer, Joy Magestro, Rose Silverstein, Sophie Borden and Tati Piskula. Special thanks also to lifelong friends Jeff Cummings and Ellin Smalley.

This wouldn't be complete without a tribute of gratitude to the memory of my late husband, Jeff Piskula, a three-star French-trained chef, and my Grandma Dot, who began teaching me how to make pies while standing on a stool at the enamel top of her Hoosier. They both placed food and family dining at the center of their lives.

Joint thanks:

We would both like to offer our thanks to the vegan community of greater Boston and beyond for sharing their knowledge, sources and resources. These include: Usha Bapna; Colette Bourassa; Sarah Bowman; Ed Cohen; Jackie Dileo; Liz Eisenberg; Didi Emmons; Nick Fountain; Clark Freifeld; Kyle Gardner; Phyllis, Lauren and Diane Garvey; Susanne Gelber; Ben Lucal; Louise Miller; Hassan Moutaouakil; Hoai Nguyen; Jim O'Hara; Virginie, Bob and Roy Palmeri; and Jenny Zimmer. Each offered expert advice from his or her uniquely informed perspective.

Our agent, Lisa Ekus, was readily available and offered steadfast support every step of the way. Thank you for being an exceptional agent and communicator. We'd also like to thank Jeff Garmel for his time and counsel at the outset of this endeavor.

At Robert Rose Inc., many creative and talented people contributed to the production of this book. Thank you first and foremost to Bob Dees for allowing us to discover, create and pursue our ideas. Judith Finlayson, our editor, provided invaluable and pragmatic solutions to the many issues that cropped up throughout the book. We are grateful for your wisdom and guidance. Jennifer MacKenzie, our recipe editor and tester, was masterful at transforming our words into clear, concise recipes. Christina Anson Mine used her considerable copyediting skills to fine-tune our manuscript, while Mark Shapiro brought our book to life with his stunning photographs with the help of food stylist Kate Bush and prop stylist Charlene Erricson. We also appreciate the contributions of the design and production team at PageWave Graphics, including Andrew Smith, Joseph Gisini, Kevin Cockburn and Daniella Zanchetta.

Introduction

WHEN WE SET OUT TO WRITE THIS BOOK, we wanted to make sure we were creating recipes that would meet the needs of today's busy families. As mothers, we understand that life is exceedingly hectic. Because we are constantly juggling the needs of kids, husbands, pets and jobs, we don't have time to spend hours over the stove as past generations of mothers were able to do. Our main objective is to prepare meals that are relatively simple yet nutritionally sound that our kids will enjoy and — with luck — request again.

With this in mind, we set out to create recipes that use ingredients people are likely to have in their pantries and that aren't too time-consuming or complicated to prepare. In pursuit of this goal we interviewed a wide circle of vegans about their food choices, meal-planning requirements and the ingredients they use most often. We also polled culinary professionals who focus on the vegan market, such as chefs and restaurateurs. Our recipes are informed by these exchanges as well as by the needs and desires of our own families. We can attest to the fact that all of the recipes in this book have met with the approval of our husbands and children (five between us). That was no easy feat, and many went through numerous revisions, but it was the litmus test before we sent any recipe out for testing.

In our experience, vegan cookbooks are often filled with recipes that contain hard-to-find ingredients or that require involved, time-consuming preparation. In contrast, our family-friendly recipes use readily available ingredients and are relatively quick and easy to prepare. They provide a well-balanced selection of classic recipes that we have adapted to veganism, as well as many international dishes that reflect today's increasingly multicultural world.

We are fortunate to live in New England, a region with a lush and diverse agricultural backdrop. As a result, from mid-June through the end of October we are able to find delicious fresh produce at our local farmers' market. Whenever possible, we use fresh ingredients rather than dried or packaged, but we recognize that this isn't always possible, a practical reality that our recipes take into account.

Whether you are single, partnered or married, or have children, you should be able to find recipes that appeal to you in this book. We hope you enjoy the book and that it becomes an indispensable part of planning your meals. Most importantly, enjoy the food and the experience of creating it!

— Maxine Effenson Chuck and Beth Gurney

The Vegan Kitchen

THERE IS LITTLE DOUBT THAT OVER the past few decades the natural foods landscape has grown dramatically. A wide range of nuts and whole grains, dairy-free milk substitutes and foods such as tofu and other soy products, which were previously difficult to find, are now commonly available in supermarkets. As a natural source of vitamins, minerals and fiber, fruits and vegetables remain a fundamental building block upon which vegan food choices can be based. They are low in calories and fat and contain phytochemicals and antioxidants, which appear to be beneficial in preventing disease.

Nowadays, vegans have ready access to many nutrient-rich foods, which makes veganism a potentially healthy lifestyle. Nutritionists tell us we should eat a balanced diet containing as many nutrients as possible. In other words, variety is one cornerstone of sound nutrition. From a vegan perspective, that means choosing a wide spectrum of whole grains, nuts, seeds and legumes, as well as fruits and vegetables. To ensure that your diet emphasizes nutrient-rich foods and is varied enough to ensure balance, you should research vegan nutrition by checking various vegan websites (see Resources, page 182) and reading about veganism. There is no better guide to a healthy life than knowledge, so be proactive, engage in the pursuit of self-knowledge and keep an open mind.

 ## STOCKING THE VEGAN KITCHEN

Fruits and vegetables are the anchors of the vegan diet and the core components of many of our recipes. They add their own distinct character and flavor as well as texture and volume to dishes in this book. All contribute vitamins, minerals and fiber, helping to ensure that your nutritional needs are met. To supplement these nutrients, our recipes also include a variety of other healthful ingredients to round out your nutritional needs.

The following list consists of the ingredients you'll need to create the recipes in this book. We have broken the list into three sections: Your Pantry, Your Refrigerator and Your Freezer. This will help you equip the three key areas of your kitchen with vegan options.

Your Pantry

Bread: A variety of breads serve as staples in the vegan diet. They can be used to create quick, nutritious meals, such as wraps and sandwiches. They also provide texture and can be used to add body or as a binder in many recipes. We prefer whole-grain varieties because they add protein and dietary fiber as well as other nutrients.

Chocolate and cocoa powder: In their purest form, chocolate and cocoa powder are suitable for vegans. However, some products contain additives and flavorings that may not meet vegan standards, so be sure to check the labels.

Coconut milk: Canned coconut milk (without preservatives) is available in most supermarkets and Asian markets. It can be used as a dairy alternative in many recipes.

Condiments: A variety of condiments that are vegan-compatible can be used to add flavor and, in some cases, nutrients to recipes. These include: Dijon mustard, ketchup, barbecue sauce, hoisin sauce, soy sauce, tamari, hot pepper sauce, chili paste, vinaigrettes, prepared horseradish, tahini and salsa.

Dried fruits: A staple in the vegan diet, dried fruits play a dual role in our recipes. They can be used to enhance flavor and to bind other ingredients together. Dried fruits that are readily available include: currants, golden raisins, dark raisins, cranberries, dates and dried apricots.

Egg replacer: This is a powdered mixture of starches, gums and leaveners, which substitutes well for eggs in many baked dishes. You may be able to find egg replacer in the baking section of some supermarkets, but it is most commonly found in natural food stores and health food stores.

Grains: Grains are a significant source of protein and fiber in the vegan diet. We use the following in our recipes.

- *bulgur:* cracked wheat that has been partially cooked
- *cracked wheat:* wheat berries cracked into small pieces
- *pearl barley:* lightly milled to retain the germ and at least two-thirds of the bran of barley groats
- *polenta or yellow cornmeal:* yellow medium-grain cornmeal is most versatile
- *quinoa:* light, with a nutty flavor and very high in protein
- *rice:* white and brown varieties, long- and short-grain (Arborio rice is necessary for making risotto)
- *rolled oats:* quick-cooking or old-fashioned, they are made from whole-grain oat groats and help lower blood cholesterol
- *whole wheat couscous:* whole-grain durum wheat flour made into tiny pasta pellets

Herbs: Herbs are loaded with healthy phytochemicals and antioxidants and are also great flavor enhancers. In our recipes, we use basil, bay leaves, chives, cilantro, ground cloves, dill, Italian parsley, mint (spearmint and peppermint), oregano, rosemary, sage, tarragon and thyme.

Legumes: As a primary source of protein, legumes (dried beans and lentils) are fundamental to the vegan diet. Most of our recipes call for canned beans because they are so convenient. However, if you have the time to soak and cook dried beans, by all means use them — they are more economical. When buying dried beans, look for wrinkle-free surfaces and bright colors. Store them in airtight containers for up to 6 months.

Preparing dried beans: Begin by soaking them in a bowl of water. As a rule, use three times as much water as beans. Often, foreign matter will float to the top. Use your fingers to sift through the beans and remove any stones or impurities. Let beans soak for 6 to 8 hours, then drain and rinse them thoroughly under cold running water. Transfer to a pot and add roughly three parts water to one part beans. (Some beans may require additional liquid, depending on factors such as age.) Bring to a boil and cook, uncovered, for 10 minutes. Reduce heat to low, cover and simmer for 1 to 2 hours or until beans are soft. Drain and rinse. If not using immediately, cover and refrigerate for up to 4 days. Cooked beans (and lentils) can also be frozen in an airtight container. They will keep frozen for up to 6 months.

Unlike most beans, lentils do not require soaking. However, they should be rinsed and combed through to remove impurities.

Here is a list of legumes we use in our recipes.

- *black beans:* a staple of Latin American cooking
- *cannellini beans:* white kidney beans, primarily used in Italian cuisine
- *chickpeas (garbanzo beans):* used in a wide array of international recipes
- *lentils:* used most commonly in soups and salads
- *navy beans:* white beans used in bean casseroles
- *pinto beans:* used in Mexican dishes, such as refried beans
- *red kidney beans:* used in soups, salads and casseroles

Noodles and pasta: Noodles and pasta are carbohydrate staples in the vegan diet. Wherever possible, look for whole-grain varieties. We use bow tie, couscous, ditalini, elbow macaroni, lasagna, orzo, penne, rice noodles, rice sticks (vermicelli), rice wrappers, spaghetti and udon noodles in our recipes. While most pasta doesn't contain eggs, it is worth checking labels to make sure the variety you're buying is egg-free.

Nuts: These are a source of protein and other nutrients in the vegan diet. We use almonds, peanuts, pecans, pistachios and walnuts in our recipes. Because they are high in healthy fats, which go rancid quickly, nuts should be stored in the freezer.

Spices: Spices play an important role in our recipes, as they impart flavor to neutral-tasting ingredients such as tofu, legumes, pastas and grains. We use the following in our recipes: adobo seasoning, ground allspice, bay leaves, cardamom, cayenne pepper, chili powder, ground cinnamon, cloves, ground cloves, crushed hot pepper flakes, ground cumin, whole cumin seeds, curry powder, fennel seeds, garlic powder, garlic salt, ground ginger, minced gingerroot, Mexican spice mixtures, ground nutmeg, onion powder, paprika, pumpkin pie spice, turmeric and vanilla bean.

Sweeteners: We have listed two categories of sweeteners: dry and wet. Depending on the recipe, the choice of dry or wet sweeteners may be based on the texture or consistency you wish to achieve. In many of our recipes, we offer choices so you can make adjustments based on your own preferences. Many people, particularly vegans and some vegetarians, tend to stay away from processed white sugars not only for health reasons but also because some companies have been known to use animal bone char in processing sugar. There are many unprocessed alternatives available.

Dry sweeteners: Demerara sugar, evaporated cane juice (sucanat), golden caster sugar, golden granulated sugar, granulated white sugar, dark and light muscovado sugar, natural cane sugar, turbinado sugar, unrefined dark soft brown sugar and unrefined light soft brown sugar.

Wet sweeteners and syrups: For flavor, texture and consistency, we use the following: applesauce, banana purée, blackstrap molasses, fancy molasses, maple syrup, puréed dates (especially Medjool dates) and corn syrup.

Vegetable stock or broth and vegan bouillon cubes: These items are essential to the vegan diet because they add flavor as well as liquid to recipes. Dry-storage cartons of good vegetable stocks are available in salted and salt-free versions. Vegan bouillon cubes are convenient but they contain a lot of salt. If you are using them in a recipe, you'll most likely have to reduce the amount of salt. Roasted vegetable broth, mushroom broth and onion broth are also available in dry-storage cartons and can be used interchangeably with regular vegetable stock.

Your Refrigerator

Cheese alternatives: Vegan alternatives to a wide variety of cheeses, including cream cheese, are available in natural food stores and some supermarkets. Just be sure to check the ingredients, as many cheese alternatives are made with casein, a protein found in milk. Another vegan concern is the coagulant: vegetable rennet is fine, but calf rennet is not.

Dairy-free beverages: A variety of dairy-free beverages can be found in most supermarkets. Most come in dry-storage cartons. These include:

Almond milk: This milk alternative is available in some well-stocked natural food stores and supermarkets in 1-quart (1 L) dry-storage cartons (plain, chocolate and vanilla flavors).

Rice milk: This dairy-free milk is available in 1-quart (1 L) dry-storage cartons and is often used because it has a lighter taste than soy milk. Note that there are rice milks that are flavored or fortified (enriched) with vitamins and minerals (plain, plain light, plain enriched, enriched chocolate or enriched vanilla), so it is important to read the labels carefully to make sure you're getting the kind you want. There is also a rice and soy blend available.

Soy creamer: This light cream replacement tastes rich but has only 1% fat.

Soy milk: Soy milk comes in 1-quart (1 L) dry-storage cartons and can also be found in the refrigerator section of your supermarket. Soy milks vary in their fat content and some are enriched like rice milks. They are also available in a variety of flavors, so it is important to read the labels carefully to ensure that you select the type and flavor your recipe requires. Choices include: plain, plain light, plain low-fat, no-fat plain, enriched plain, vanilla, enriched vanilla and chocolate.

Soy bacon: This product is found in the refrigerated section of the supermarket, where specialty foods and many Asian foods are located. It has the smoky, full-flavored taste you expect from real bacon.

Soy ground meat alternative: This type of soy "meat" is good for recipes that require you to shape it into patties or meatballs. It is found in the refrigerated section with tofu and other meat alternatives, such as veggie hot dogs and soy bacon.

Soy margarine and/or buttery spreads: As alternatives to butter, margarine and buttery spreads are necessary for baking and cooking. Both are available in tubs or sticks — the only difference is that the tubs have a higher moisture content. For health purposes, it is advisable to check the sodium content of any margarine or spread as well as the type of fat it contains. Do not buy any with the word *hydrogenated* on the label, as these contain unhealthy trans fats.

Soy mayonnaise: An egg-free alternative to traditional mayonnaise, this comes in regular and low-fat versions.

Tofu: Tofu is an integral part of the vegan diet. It's a good source of protein, and we use it in a wide variety of ways in our recipes. Types of tofu include:

Baked and marinated tofu: Many varieties of packaged tofu come ready to eat, seasoned and baked. They are found in the refrigerated section of some supermarkets and can be used to add taste and texture to recipes. Flavors include but are not limited to: Asian, Caribbean, Italian, smoked barbecue, spicy barbecue, ginger and sesame, smoked herb, smoked sea vegetable, smoked Thai, Roma tomato and basil, sesame peanut and zesty lemon pepper.

Extra-firm tofu: This is the tofu of choice for grilling or for use in dishes that require a pronounced presence. It will hold up to a lot of handling.

Firm tofu: Firm tofu gives body and bulk to dishes and soaks up the flavors in marinades and sauces.

Silken tofu: Silken tofu comes in a range of firmnesses, from soft to extra-firm. Silken and soft tofu are most commonly used for dips, smoothies, spreads and baked goods that require a smooth binder.

Vegan sour cream alternative: Dairy-free sour cream made from soy products is the vegan alternative to regular. It can be found in some major supermarket chains or natural food stores.

Your Freezer

Many vegan-friendly products can be kept in the freezer to make life more convenient. These include soy ground meat alternatives; vegan meat-free burgers; soy sausages; meatless meatballs (classic and Italian); frozen fruits and vegetables, including vegetable medleys, which are great for stir-frying (we particularly like organic fruits and vegetables available in some markets); and phyllo dough sheets. Always make sure to read labels, as there may be some unexpected, nonvegan ingredients.

COOKING TERMS AND TECHNIQUES

Blanching: This technique is used to preserve the outside color and to partially cook vegetables. When blanching vegetables, submerge them in a pot of rapidly boiling salted water. Keep the pot uncovered. When the water returns to a boil, remove the vegetables with a slotted spoon and plunge them into ice water.

Bouquet garni: This is a French term for a bundle of seasonings that is usually wrapped in cheesecloth and tied with kitchen string. A basic bouquet garni is made of one bay leaf, a few sprigs of parsley (including stems) and a few sprigs of fresh thyme.

Cutting terms: There are a number of terms that are commonly used to indicate how ingredients should be cut.

Chopping and dicing: There is a small distinction between chopping and dicing. Chopping does not refer to shape, whereas dicing refers to cutting food into pieces that are approximately cube-shaped.

Finely chopping or finely dicing: To chop or dice food into pieces about $\frac{1}{8}$ to $\frac{1}{6}$ inch (0.25 to 0.40 cm) in size.

Medium chopping or medium dicing: To chop or dice food into pieces $\frac{1}{6}$ inch to $\frac{1}{2}$ inch (0.40 cm to 1 cm).

Coarsely chopping or coarsely dicing: To chop or dice food into pieces larger than $\frac{1}{2}$ inch (1 cm).

Grating: Grating involves scraping food against a metal or plastic grater to produce coarse, medium or fine shreds.

Finely grate: To grate using the finest holes on a grater.

Grate: To grate using the medium holes on a grater.

Coarsely grate: To grate using the largest holes on a grater.

Mincing: Finely chopping food into small flecks or particles. This allows flavors to permeate a recipe and keeps the texture fairly consistent. (Note: Although you can use a garlic press to crush garlic, we believe that mincing garlic by hand with a knife results in the best flavor.)

Slicing: Slicing refers to a method of cutting food into parallel, uniform slices.

Finely slice: To slice to approximately $\frac{1}{8}$ to $\frac{1}{6}$ inch (0.25 to 0.40 cm) thickness.

Slice: To slice to approximately $\frac{1}{4}$ to $\frac{1}{3}$ inch (0.5 to 0.75 cm) thickness.

Developing flavor: There are various ways to develop fuller and deeper flavors. We use the following methods in our recipes.

Infusing, steeping or brewing: These terms describe methods for developing flavor by placing ingredients in a hot liquid and letting them stand for a period of time (tea leaves in hot water, or a vanilla bean in hot syrup).

Making marinades and dressings: To extract the deepest flavor when making a marinade, dressing or sauce, begin with vinegar or citrus juice and add the herbs or spices before the oil.

Roasting or baking vegetables: Roasting or baking vegetables in a washed, unpeeled state retains the nutrients located just under the surface of the skin. For this reason, we encourage you, whenever possible, to leave skins on fruits and vegetables.

Using marinades and dressings: Many ingredients are more receptive to dressings, marinades and seasonings when they are hot. We suggest that you prepare your dressing or marinade while grains, beans, pasta or starchy vegetables are cooking so you can immediately submerge or toss them together after cooking.

Folding: This technique allows you to combine ingredients in a way that will keep the mixture light. To do this, carefully insert a rubber spatula and lift ingredients from the bottom upward, repeating the process as you turn the bowl. Unlike stirring or beating, this allows you to combine ingredients without losing air in the mixture.

Juicing citrus fruits: To extract the juice of a citrus fruit, bear down on the fruit with the palm of your hand and roll it around on a clean, firm surface for 1 minute. This helps break down the membranes and tissues as it releases the juices. Then, cut the fruit in half and squeeze over a receptacle or use a juicer. Use a strainer to remove pulp and seeds.

Making bread crumbs: There are two kinds of bread crumbs: fresh and dry. To make fresh bread crumbs, use a food processor to pulse pieces of fresh bread. To make dry bread crumbs, use stale bread or toast fresh bread. When toast is cool, grind in a food processor or blender until it is the desired texture.

Measuring dry ingredients: To measure dry ingredients correctly, it is important to avoid shaking or packing down the ingredients. To ensure consistent results, lightly spoon ingredients into a dry measuring cup or spoon, then level off the top with a knife.

Measuring fresh herbs or equivalent dry herbs: One tbsp (15 mL) of a chopped fresh herb is equivalent to one tsp (5 mL) of a crushed or chopped dried herb. A pinch or a dash is a scant amount equal to approximately $\frac{1}{8}$ tsp (0.5 mL). A pinch is used for dry ingredients and a dash refers to those that are wet.

Mixing ingredients: In baking, texture is critical. When combining dry flour mixtures with liquids, it is possible to develop a stringy protein known as gluten, which makes baked goods tough. When making dough for baked goods other than yeast breads, keep mixing to a minimum. The terminology "just until combined" and "do not overbeat" are ways of telling you how to keep the texture tender.

Peeling and seeding tomatoes: *To peel tomatoes:* Using a paring knife, make an X in the bottom of the fruit. Carefully lower tomatoes into rapidly boiling water, two at a time. Remove tomatoes with a slotted spoon after 30 seconds. Immediately submerge them in a bowl of ice water (or very cold water). The skins will naturally separate from the flesh. Cut the stem section out with a paring knife. *To seed tomatoes:* Cut tomatoes in half crosswise (like the equator) rather than from stem to base. Gently squeeze out the seeds. Use your index finger to scoop out any seeds that may be hiding.

Preventing discoloration of fruits: Adding an acid, such as citrus juice or vinegar, to many white-fleshed fruits prevents them from browning.

Removing baked goods from the oven: Baked goods removed from the oven need to release steam from their interiors before they are unmolded. Cooling them in the pan on an elevated wire rack for 8 to 10 minutes allows them to solidify and keep their form when they're unmolded.

Serving temperatures: The texture of vegan dishes is not compromised due to temperature fluctuations the way it is in animal- and/or dairy-based dishes. There is less separation of saturated fat and less concern about cross-contamination due to salmonella. As a result, there are more recipes that lend themselves to being served at any temperature.

Testing for doneness: The test for doneness varies based on what you are testing.

For baked fruits: Raw fruit renders its juices into bubbling sauces in the case of pies and crisps. Using a fork or skewer, test for resistance. The fruit is done if it is tender and offers no resistance. A deep, rich aroma is also indicative of doneness.

For baked goods: The usual test is to pierce the center of a baked item with a skewer to see if any uncooked batter clings to the tester when removed. This is helpful, but we do not strictly rely on this test the way traditional recipes do. In egg-free baking, we do not have the same concerns about texture and cross-contamination. Another method is testing by touch, in which you either press the center of the surface with the back of a spoon or your finger. If it retains the depression, it must continue to cook. If it bounces back, it's done.

For pasta and grains: Sampling a small taste of grains or pasta is the best way to test for doneness; they should be firm but tender. Risottos are classically done to an "al dente" texture, in which the center of the grain is just barely cooked and firmer than the outer part of the grain. When cooking rice, it is done when all liquid is absorbed and the grains are cooked evenly throughout.

For vegetables: The easiest method for testing whether vegetables are done is to pierce them with a fork to feel their tenderness. You can also taste a sample.

Tofu: *To measure tofu:* The most accurate way to measure tofu is the water displacement method. Place cubes of tofu in a premeasured amount of water and measure by the volume of water that is displaced. For example, if a recipe calls for $\frac{1}{2}$ cup (125 mL) tofu, fill a 1-cup (250 mL) measure with $\frac{1}{2}$ cup (125 mL) water. Add tofu cubes until the water reaches the 1-cup (250 mL) mark.

To freeze tofu: Firm and extra-firm tofu can be frozen. Cut tofu into cubes, then place in storage bags and freeze. Defrosted tofu has a drier texture than fresh.

To press tofu: Firm and extra-firm tofu can be pressed to extract excess water. Cut the tofu as the recipe instructs, then place it on a paper towel–lined plate. Cover with another paper towel and place a plate on top. Add a weight (a bowl of water works well) to the plate and set aside for 20 to 30 minutes. Drain off excess liquid and use tofu in recipe.

To preserve tofu: When storing tofu in the refrigerator, drain it daily and cover with fresh water. Store in an airtight container. This does not apply to marinated and baked tofu, which have been dehydrated.

Appetizers

This versatile spread has many applications. Serve it as an appetizer with sliced vegetables, as a dip for crackers or in a pita. It can be stored, tightly covered, in the refrigerator for 3 or 4 days.

Tips

Because can sizes vary, we provide a range of amounts for beans in our recipes. If you're using the larger size, you may want to adjust the seasoning by adding a pinch of cumin and salt.

You can use bottled roasted red bell peppers in this hummus or roast your own (see Roasted Bell Peppers, page 151).

Hummus with Roasted Red Peppers

✎ *Food processor or blender*

1	can (14 to 19 oz/398 to 540 mL) chickpeas, drained and rinsed (see Tips, left), or 1 cup (250 mL) dried chickpeas, soaked, cooked and drained (see Legumes, page 13)	1
¼ cup	tahini	50 mL
¼ cup	freshly squeezed lemon juice	50 mL
2	cloves garlic, minced	2
Half	roasted red bell pepper, peeled and thinly sliced (see Tips, left)	Half
1 tsp	ground cumin	5 mL
¼ tsp	salt, or to taste	1 mL
	Water, optional	

1. In food processor or blender, combine chickpeas, tahini, lemon juice and garlic and process until smooth.

2. Add roasted red peppers, ground cumin and salt and process until smooth. If you prefer a creamier consistency, add water, 1 tbsp (15 mL) at a time, processing until the desired texture is achieved.

3. Transfer to an airtight container and refrigerate for at least 2 hours or overnight.

Variations

Hummus with Black Olives: Substitute ½ cup (125 mL) chopped pitted kalamata olives for the red pepper.

Lemony Hummus: Substitute 1 tbsp (15 mL) grated lemon zest for the red pepper.

Versatile Peanut Dip

We particularly enjoy the rich Asian-inspired flavors of this dipping sauce with fresh vegetables such as carrots, broccoli, bell peppers and celery, but we call this dip versatile because it can also be used as a sauce in main courses, too (see Variations, below).

Tips

Lapsang Souchong tea is a deeply flavored smoky Chinese black tea. It adds a particularly nice dimension to this sauce. If you don't have it in your cupboard, regular black tea works well, too.

You can substitute ¼ tsp (1 mL) hot pepper flakes for the chili paste. Add to the hot tea and allow to steep for 1 minute before adding to the peanut butter mixture.

In many locations, green onions are known as scallions.

If the dip has been refrigerated, for the best consistency let it return to room temperature before serving.

½ cup	smooth natural peanut butter	125 mL
3 tbsp	packed light brown sugar or other dry sweetener (see Sweeteners, page 14)	45 mL
½ cup	hot brewed black tea, such as Lapsang Souchong (see Tips, left)	125 mL
2 tbsp	low-sodium soy sauce	25 mL
½ tsp	chili paste	2 mL
3	green onions (green and white parts), thinly sliced (see Tips, left)	3
3 tbsp	coarsely chopped salted roasted peanuts	45 mL
1 tbsp	chopped fresh basil leaves (or 1 tsp/5 mL dried)	15 mL
	Fresh cilantro leaves, coarsely chopped, optional	

1. In a bowl, whisk peanut butter with brown sugar until blended. Add hot tea, soy sauce and chili paste. Mix well. Add green onions, peanuts and basil and mix until blended.

2. Transfer to a small serving bowl, cover and refrigerate. Just before serving, garnish with cilantro, if using.

Variations

Add ½ tsp (2 mL) ground cumin along with the soy sauce.

This tasty dip can also enhance main-course dishes such as Veggie Kabobs (see recipe, page 144). It also makes a great main course tossed with plain pasta or any Asian noodle of your choice.

... these make delicious hors d'oeuvres when cut into quarters, you can also serve them whole with a salad as a main course for four.

Tips

To drain thawed frozen spinach, place it in a fine-mesh strainer and press down with a wooden spoon until all the moisture is removed. If you don't have a fine-mesh strainer, you can use your hands. Working with a small handful of spinach at a time, gently squeeze four or five times to remove excess liquid. Repeat until all the spinach has been drained.

These mushroom caps can be frozen for up to 1 month. Reheat directly from the freezer in a 400°F (200°C) oven for 15 minutes.

Stuffed Portobello Mushroom Caps

➣ Preheat oven to 375°F (190°C)
➣ Baking sheet, greased

2 tbsp	dried currants	25 mL
2 tbsp	minced shallot	25 mL
2 tbsp	balsamic vinegar	25 mL
2 tbsp	water	25 mL
1 1/2 tbsp	prepared Italian salad dressing	22 mL
4	portobello mushrooms (each about 4 inches/10 cm in diameter), stems removed and set aside	4
	Salt and freshly ground black pepper, optional	
1/3 cup	walnut pieces	75 mL
1	package (10 oz/300 g) frozen chopped spinach, thawed and drained (see Tips, left)	1
4 oz	vegan cream cheese–style spread	125 g
	Salt and freshly ground black pepper	

1. In a small saucepan over medium–high heat, combine currants, shallot, balsamic vinegar and water. Heat for 2 minutes or until currants are plump and shallot is softened. Pour cooking liquid into a small bowl and set currant mixture aside. Add Italian dressing to cooking liquid and mix well. Lightly brush mushrooms with Italian dressing mixture, ensuring that all surfaces are evenly coated. Place on prepared baking sheet, gill side up. Set remaining dressing mixture aside.

2. Finely chop the reserved mushroom stems and distribute evenly among the caps. Season with salt and pepper to taste, if using. Sprinkle walnut pieces over baking sheet. Bake in preheated oven for 8 minutes or until walnuts are lightly toasted and mushrooms are slightly tender. Remove from oven.

3. In a medium bowl, combine spinach and vegan cream cheese. Mash with a fork until blended. Add remaining dressing mixture, reserved shallots and currants, and toasted walnut pieces; mash until combined. Season with salt and pepper to taste.

4. Using a soupspoon, fill mushroom caps with spinach mixture. Pack tightly and evenly to form a dome. Return mushrooms to oven for 18 minutes or until heated through. Remove from oven and immediately brush with any pan juices. Let cool for 5 minutes. Cut into quarters and serve.

Variation

Substitute pine nuts for the walnuts, and/or golden or dark raisins for the dried currants. You can also add ½ tsp (2 mL) of your favorite dried herb and/or one clove garlic, finely minced, to the spinach mixture.

Spinach Dip

This adaptable dip is a perfect accompaniment to sliced vegetables, bread or crackers. For an attractive presentation, hollow out a round loaf of bread and spoon the dip into the cavity. Cut the hollowed-out bread into bite-size pieces and use them for dipping.

Tips

To drain thawed frozen spinach, place it in a fine-mesh strainer and press down with a wooden spoon until all the moisture is removed. If you don't have a fine-mesh strainer, you can use your hands. Working with a small handful of spinach at a time, gently squeeze four or five times to remove excess liquid. Repeat until all the spinach has been drained. For this recipe, you should have about 1 cup (250 mL) spinach when you are finished.

In many locations, green onions are known as scallions.

1 cup	soy mayonnaise	250 mL
1 cup	vegan sour cream alternative	250 mL
½ cup	coarsely chopped green onions (white and green parts), see Tips, left	125 mL
4	cloves garlic, minced (about 4 tsp/20 mL)	4
1 tbsp	freshly squeezed lemon juice	15 mL
1 tsp	prepared Italian salad dressing	5 mL
1	package (10 oz/300 g) frozen chopped spinach, thawed and drained (see Tips, left)	1

1. In a bowl, combine soy mayonnaise and vegan sour cream. Add green onions, garlic, lemon juice and Italian salad dressing and blend well. Add spinach and mix thoroughly. Cover and refrigerate until chilled, about an hour.

Variation

For a particularly striking presentation, serve this dip in a clear glass bowl, surrounded by a ring of sliced red peppers.

Eggplant and Olive Dip

This recipe has such an involved history. We're not sure exactly whose friend gave it to whose friend but we think it originated in Arizona or California. It has always been a favorite, and over the years we've updated it several times. It's a great vehicle for inspiring an eggplant-averse individual to rethink his or her relationship with this vegetable. We like to serve this dip with pita, crackers or sliced vegetables.

Tips

You'll need about 2½ lbs (1.25 kg) of eggplant for this recipe.

Use one-and-a-half 6-oz (175 g) cans of tomato paste to make 1 cup (250 mL).

Look for natural cane sugar in the baking section of natural food stores and many large supermarket chains. If you prefer, use another dry sweetener (see page 14).

This dip can do double duty as a plated appetizer. Just spoon the chilled dip onto a bed of lettuce.

2	medium eggplant, peeled and cut into 1-inch (2.5 cm) cubes	2
3 tbsp	kosher or coarse sea salt	45 mL
½ cup	olive oil	125 mL
2	medium yellow onions, finely chopped	2
4	cloves garlic, minced (about 4 tsp/20 mL)	4
1	red bell pepper, cut into ¼-inch (0.5 cm) strips, then cut in half	1
2 cups	thinly sliced mushrooms	500 mL
1 cup	tomato paste (see Tips, left)	250 mL
½ cup	water (approx)	125 mL
⅓ cup	red wine vinegar	75 mL
1 cup	pimiento-stuffed green olives	250 mL
2 tbsp	capers, rinsed and drained	25 mL
2 tbsp	fresh oregano leaves, finely chopped (or 2 tsp/10 mL dried)	25 mL
1 tbsp	natural cane sugar (see Tips, left)	15 mL
½ tsp	table salt or fine sea salt	2 mL
¼ tsp	freshly ground black pepper	1 mL

1. In a colander over a sink, toss eggplant with salt. Let drain for 20 minutes. Rinse and pat dry.

2. In a large skillet, heat oil for 1 minute over medium heat. Add onions and cook, stirring, for 3 minutes or until softened. Add garlic and cook, stirring, for 1 minute. Add eggplant and cook, stirring, for 4 minutes or until eggplant begins to soften. Stir in red pepper and mushrooms. Reduce heat to low, cover and cook for 5 minutes.

3. Add tomato paste, water and red wine vinegar. Mix well. Add more water, 1 tbsp (15 mL) at a time, if mixture is too thick. Stir in olives, capers, oregano, natural cane sugar, salt and pepper. Simmer, uncovered, for 20 minutes, stirring occasionally, until the flavors meld.

4. Let cool for 5 minutes. Transfer to a bowl, cover and refrigerate for 1 hour or until thoroughly chilled.

Variations

If you like a bit of spice, add ½ tsp (2 mL) hot pepper flakes along with the oregano.

Replace pimiento-stuffed green olives with a mixture of pitted green and black olives.

Chunky Guacamole

Tips

Use 1 tbsp (15 mL) finely
chopped pickled jalapeño
peppers if fresh are not
available. The added
vinegar in the peppers will
alter the taste slightly, so
taste before adding the full
tablespoon (15 mL) of
pickled peppers.

People have different
preferences regarding the
consistency of guacamole.
If you prefer a smoother
consistency, make it in a
food processor for
convenience.

2	avocados, peeled, pitted and quartered	2
2	cloves garlic, minced (about 2 tsp/10 mL)	2
1	small tomato, seeded and finely diced	1
1 ½ tsp	freshly squeezed lime juice	7 mL
1	jalapeño pepper, seeded and finely chopped, optional (see Tips, left)	1
½ tsp	hot pepper sauce, or to taste	2 mL
	Salt and freshly ground black pepper	

1. In a bowl, using a fork or potato masher, mash avocados until the desired consistency is reached (see Tips, left). Add garlic, tomato, lime juice, jalapeño pepper, if using, and hot pepper sauce. Mix well and season with salt and freshly ground black pepper to taste. Serve immediately or cover and chill. Guacamole is best eaten within a day.

Tomato and Garlic Salsa

Tips

This salsa is best eaten within 4 days.

In many locations, green onions are known as scallions.

1	can (28 oz/796 mL) diced tomatoes, with juices	1
	Juice of 1 lime	
¼ cup	fresh cilantro leaves, coarsely chopped	50 mL
2	cloves garlic, minced	2
¼ cup	finely chopped sweet onion, such as Vidalia	50 mL
¼ cup	coarsely chopped green onions (white and green parts), see Tips, left	50 mL
1	jalapeño pepper, seeded and finely chopped, optional	1
1 tsp	natural cane sugar or other dry sweetener	5 mL
1 tsp	distilled white vinegar	5 mL
	Salt and freshly ground black pepper	

1. In a bowl, combine tomatoes, lime juice, cilantro, garlic, sweet onion, green onions, jalapeño pepper, if using, sugar and vinegar. Mix well. Season to taste with salt and freshly ground black pepper.

2. Cover and refrigerate for 2 to 3 hours or until chilled and flavors are blended.

Variation

Vary this recipe to suit your taste. We often add hot pepper sauce on its own or along with ¼ cup (50 mL) cooked corn kernels or half a medium green bell pepper, finely diced.

These turnovers make a great dinner dish as well as an hors d'oeuvre. Beth's daughters enjoy helping her fill and seal them as an antidote to predinner boredom. The turnovers freeze well, uncooked, for up to 3 months, so you can make more than you'll need for one occasion and enjoy the remainder at a later date.

Tips

Cool the turnover filling until it is slightly warm, but not so warm that it distorts the wonton wrapper.

Stove elements and skillets are likely to have hot spots. Rotate the turnovers from the middle to the outer edge of the skillet and vice versa when turning them to ensure they cook evenly.

Leftover wonton wrappers can be wrapped tightly in plastic and frozen for 3 months. Frozen turnovers should be thawed before cooking. To cook and serve, see steps 3 and 4.

Asian Vegetable Turnovers

🍃 *Preheat oven to 275°F (140°C)*

1 tbsp	sesame oil	15 mL
1	large shallot, thinly sliced (about ¼ cup/50 mL)	1
1	large portobello mushroom, cut in ¼-inch (0.5 cm) dice, or other mushrooms, thinly sliced (about 1½ cups/375 mL)	1
1	medium carrot, peeled and grated	1
2 cups	thinly sliced cabbage	500 mL
1 cup	bean sprouts	250 mL
⅓ cup	fresh Asian or Italian basil leaves, coarsely chopped (or 1½ tbsp/22 mL dried)	75 mL
1 tbsp	low-sodium soy sauce	15 mL
1 tbsp	rice vinegar	15 mL
¼ tsp	chili paste or hot pepper flakes	1 mL
1	package (1 lb/500 g) round rice wonton wrappers, about 3 inches (7.5 cm) in diameter	1
	Vegetable oil for frying	

DIPPING SAUCE

½ cup	low-sodium soy sauce	125 mL
⅓ cup	packed brown sugar	75 mL
2 tsp	sesame oil	10 mL
½ tsp	chili paste	2 mL

1. Heat a large skillet over medium heat for 30 seconds. Add sesame oil, turning the pan to coat it thoroughly. Add shallot and cook, stirring, for 1 minute or until softened. Add mushroom and cook, stirring, for 1 minute. Stir in carrot and cabbage. Increase heat to medium–high and cook, stirring, for 3 minutes or until vegetables are softened. Stir in bean sprouts, basil, soy sauce, rice vinegar and chili paste. Lower heat to medium and cook, stirring, for 1 minute or until the bean sprouts have lost their crunch and the seasonings have blended. Transfer to a bowl and set aside until mixture is cool enough to handle (see Tips, left).

2. Working with a few wrappers at a time and keeping the remainder covered to prevent them from drying out, place wrappers on a clean work surface. Place 1 tsp (5 mL) of the vegetable mixture in the middle of each wrap. Lightly brush a ½-inch (1 cm) border around one half of the edge of each wrapper with water. Fold opposite edge over filling to make a half-moon shape. Press and crimp wet edge against dry edge to seal. Place the turnovers on a plate. Repeat until all the wrappers and/or filling have been used up.

3. Fill a large skillet with vegetable oil to a depth of ½ inch (1 cm). Heat over medium-high heat until hot but not smoking. (It has reached the right temperature when a piece of wonton wrapper sizzles when dropped into the oil.) In batches, in skillet, arrange turnovers in a single layer, evenly spaced. Cook, turning once, for 4 minutes per side or until well browned. Drain on paper towels and keep warm in preheated oven until ready to serve.

4. *Dipping sauce:* In a small bowl, mix together soy sauce, brown sugar, sesame oil and chili paste. Arrange cooked turnovers on a plate around a bowl of sauce.

Variation

For a more substantial dish, add a ½-inch (1 cm) cube of silken tofu to the center of each turnover before sealing it.

These tasty nibbles are a mouthful of lively flavors and a crowd-pleaser for any occasion.

Tips

Use prepared guacamole and/or salsa or make your own (see Chunky Guacamole, page 28, and Tomato and Garlic Salsa, page 29).

Adjust the spiciness of these nachos by using mild, medium or hot salsa.

Layered Nachos

❧ Preheat oven to 475°F (240°C)
❧ Large rimmed baking sheet, ungreased

1	bag tortilla chips (8 oz/250 g)	1
2/3 cup	refried beans (approx)	150 mL
2/3 cup	guacamole (approx), see Tips, left	150 mL
2/3 cup	salsa (see Tips, left)	150 mL
3/4 cup	shredded vegan Cheddar cheese alternative	175 mL

1. Place tortilla chips in a single layer on baking sheet. On each chip, spread a thin layer of refried beans, then a thin layer of guacamole, using enough beans and guacamole to cover chips. Top each chip with a thin layer of salsa. Sprinkle shredded cheese liberally over each chip. Bake for 5 to 7 minutes or until nachos are heated through.

2. Let cool for 5 minutes or until the nachos are cool enough handle.

Spinach Dip (page 26), Hummus with Roasted Red Peppers (page 22) and Herbed Flatbread Chips (page 37)

Spicy Black Bean Dip

Serve this flavorful dip with a fresh vegetable platter or tortilla chips for a great appetizer. It also does double duty as a sandwich spread.

Tips

Use prepared salsa or make your own (see Tomato and Garlic Salsa, page 29). Your dip will be as spicy as the salsa you use. If you want additional heat, add a few drops of hot pepper sauce and/or finely chopped fresh jalapeño peppers (seeds and ribs removed), to taste.

Make this dip in a food processor for convenience. Process beans to the desired texture, then add garlic, cumin, chili powder and salsa and pulse until blended.

Because can sizes vary, we provide a range of amounts for beans in our recipes. If you're using the larger size, you may want to adjust the seasoning by adding a pinch of cumin and chili powder.

1	can (14 to 19 oz/398 mL to 540 mL) black beans, drained and rinsed (see Tips, left), or 1 cup (250 mL) dried black beans, soaked, cooked and drained (see Legumes, page 13)	1
2	cloves garlic, minced (about 2 tsp/10 mL)	2
1 tsp	ground cumin	5 mL
½ tsp	chili powder	2 mL
½ cup	salsa (see Tips, left)	125 mL

1. In a bowl, using a potato masher or fork, mash beans until fairly smooth. Add garlic, cumin and chili powder and mix well. Add salsa and mix well.

2. Cover and refrigerate for at least 2 hours or until chilled.

*Fresh Minted Pea Soup
(page 52)*

This appetizer is pleasing year-round. These bite-size mushroom triangles keep well in the freezer, so you can have them on hand for unexpected guests. Pop them out of the freezer and they are ready to serve in just minutes.

Tips

When buying phyllo for this recipe, check the size of the sheets. Most phyllo comes in sheets that are roughly 14 by 9 inches (35 by 22.5 cm), which produce three strips, each 3 inches (7.5 cm) wide. However, some sheets are 13 by 18 inches (32.5 by 45 cm), which will produce six strips of that width. Phyllo usually comes in a 1-lb (500 g) package that contains two 8-oz (250 g) rolls. You will need to thaw only one for this recipe. If you have the larger sheets, cut each into six strips. You may have only 20 sheets in your roll, which might leave you with a bit of excess filling.

These unbaked triangles can be double-wrapped in plastic wrap and frozen in layers for up to 2 months. To bake from frozen, place triangles on an ungreased baking sheet in a preheated oven and proceed with Step 6. Pierce center of one triangle with a fork to test for doneness. After piercing the triangle, touch the fork with your finger to make sure the center is heated through.

Mushrooms in a Blanket

❧*Preheat oven to 375°F (190°C)*

2 tbsp	dried currants or coarsely chopped raisins	25 mL
2 tbsp	balsamic vinegar	25 mL
3/4 cup	olive oil, divided	175 mL
2	leeks (white and light green parts only), washed, drained and cut in 1/4-inch (0.5 cm) slices	2
1 lb	mixed fresh mushrooms, cut in 1/4-inch (0.5 cm) slices	500 g
1 tsp	chopped fresh rosemary leaves (or 1/4 tsp/1 mL dried)	5 mL
Pinch	each salt and freshly ground black pepper	Pinch
1 tbsp	finely chopped fresh Italian parsley	15 mL
8 oz	phyllo sheets, thawed (approx), see Tips, left	250 g

1. In a small saucepan, cook currants with balsamic vinegar over medium heat for 1 minute. Remove from heat and set aside.

2. In a large skillet, heat 2 tbsp (25 mL) olive oil over medium heat for 1 minute. Add leeks and cook, stirring often, for 6 to 8 minutes or until softened. Add reserved currant mixture, sliced mushrooms, rosemary, salt and pepper. Cook, stirring often, for 12 to 15 minutes or until the mushroom liquid is evaporated. Remove from heat and stir in parsley. Let mixture cool to room temperature.

3. Place one sheet of phyllo on work surface, keeping remaining phyllo under a moist (but not wet) towel to prevent it from drying out. Cut sheet into three strips, each measuring about 13 by 3 inches (32.5 by 7.5 cm), see Tips, left. Lay out one strip of phyllo in a north to south position. Brush it with a little of the remaining olive oil. Add two more strips of phyllo, brushing each with olive oil after adding to previous layer. Each strip will have a total of three layers.

4. Place 1 tbsp (15 mL) of the mushroom mixture at the top edge of the strip. Fold both top corners to completely cover the filling, then begin to roll it fairly tightly toward you, using up about 4 inches (10 cm) of the strip. Fold the rolled phyllo from the upper right across and down to the left edge, forming a triangle. Continue folding triangle down and across in this manner to the bottom of the strip.

5. Place triangle, seam side down, on baking sheet. Lightly brush finished triangle with oil. Repeat with remaining phyllo, oil and filling, keeping finished triangles 1 inch (2.5 cm) apart on baking sheet and adding more phyllo sheets to use up extra filling, if desired.

6. Bake in preheated oven for 10 minutes or until golden. Using a metal spatula, turn each triangle over. Cook for 5 minutes longer or until both sides are evenly browned. Let cool for 2 to 3 minutes before serving.

Variation

Substitute four large shallots for the leeks.

This dip blends the luscious flavors of rosemary, roasted garlic and lemon. It is particularly delicious served with Herbed Flatbread Chips (see recipe, page 37), crackers or fresh vegetables. It is also good in a pita, wrap or sandwich with lettuce, tomatoes and roasted peppers.

Tips

To store roasted garlic, wrap loosely in foil, place in a plastic bag, seal tightly and refrigerate. To use, squeeze cloves out of their skins and add to sauces, soups, stews, dressings and dips.

If you prefer a coarser texture, make this dip by hand using a fork or potato masher.

Because can sizes vary, we provide a range of amounts for beans in our recipes. If you're using the larger size, you may want to adjust the seasoning by adding an additional pinch of crushed dried rosemary and cayenne pepper.

Roasted Garlic and White Bean Dip

❧*Preheat oven to 375°F (190°C)*
❧*Food processor or blender*

ROASTED GARLIC

1	head garlic	1
	Olive oil	

WHITE BEAN DIP

1	can (14 to 19 oz/398 to 540 mL) cannellini (white kidney) beans, drained and rinsed, or 1 cup (250 mL) dried cannellini beans, soaked, cooked and drained (see Legumes, page 13)	1
¼ tsp	dried rosemary leaves, crushed	1 mL
⅛ tsp	finely grated lemon zest	0.5 mL
1 tsp	freshly squeezed lemon juice	5 mL
1 tsp	olive oil	5 mL
½ tsp	red wine vinegar	2 mL
Pinch	cayenne pepper	Pinch
	Salt, optional	

1. *Roasted garlic:* Slice the top ¼ inch (0.5 cm) off garlic head, keeping the head intact and exposing a small piece of each clove. Place the garlic head in the middle of an 8-inch (20 cm) square of foil and drizzle with olive oil, coating it evenly. Fold up the corners of the foil and pinch them together to make a teardrop shape. Bake in preheated oven for 40 minutes or until garlic is soft and fragrant. Let cool. Squeeze five cloves out of their skins and set aside. Store remainder for another use (see Tips, left).

2. *White bean dip:* In food processor, combine reserved garlic, beans, rosemary and lemon zest and pulse eight to 10 times. Add lemon juice, olive oil and red wine vinegar and pulse until desired consistency is achieved. Add cayenne pepper, and salt to taste, if using, and pulse three or four times. Transfer to a serving bowl and serve immediately or cover and chill overnight.

Variation
Replace rosemary with ½ tsp (2 mL) dried basil, oregano, sage or thyme.

These homemade crackers have enough personality to stand on their own but they also go well with Roasted Garlic and White Bean Dip (see recipe, page 36) and Olive Spread (see recipe, page 39).

Tips

Pitas vary in thickness; some have sides that are twice as thick as others. If this is the case, remove thin chips from the pan with a metal spatula as they are done, leaving the thicker ones to cook longer.

In many locations, green onions are known as scallions.

These chips can be stored in an airtight container for up to 1 week.

Herbed Flatbread Chips

✎ *Preheat oven to 375°F (190°C)*
✎ *Large rimmed baking sheet, ungreased*

6	whole wheat pitas (each about 1 oz/30 g)	6
¼ cup	olive oil	50 mL
2 tbsp	minced green onion (white and light green parts only)	25 mL
1 tbsp	chopped fresh basil leaves (or 1 tsp/5mL dried)	15 mL
¼ tsp	fine sea salt	1 mL
¼ tsp	freshly ground black pepper	1 mL

1. Cut pitas into quarters. Separate the top and bottom pieces. Place on baking sheet in a single layer, without overlapping if possible. Lightly brush with olive oil and sprinkle evenly with green onion, basil, salt and pepper.

2. Bake in preheated oven for 8 to 12 minutes or until light brown and crisp. Let cool on pan for 5 minutes before serving or storing (see Tips, left).

Variation

Use 1 tsp (5 mL) garlic salt instead of sea salt, flavored oils instead of olive oil or any herb of your choice instead of basil, following the proportions in this recipe.

---

*These pecans are a tasty
snack on their own or
a crunchy garnish for salads
and even desserts. They
keep for up to 1 month
in a well-sealed airtight
container. Caution: They
can be addictive!*

Tip

To keep the pecans crisp
and dry, store in an airtight
container at room
temperature.

Spicy Pecans

❧ *Preheat oven to 375°F (190°C)*
❧ *Large rimmed baking sheet, ungreased*

3 cups	pecan halves	750 mL
¼ cup	packed light brown sugar or granulated natural cane sugar	50 mL
2 tsp	salt	10 mL
1 tsp	cayenne pepper	5 mL
1 tsp	paprika	5 mL
¾ tsp	ground ginger	3 mL
¼ cup	pure maple syrup	50 mL
1 tbsp	water	15 mL
2 tsp	vegetable oil	10 mL
½ tsp	finely grated orange zest	2 mL

1. Spread pecan halves in a single layer on baking sheet. Bake in preheated oven for 8 to 10 minutes or until toasted and fragrant.

2. In a bowl, mix together sugar, salt, cayenne, paprika and ginger. Set aside.

3. In a saucepan, combine maple syrup, water, oil and orange zest. Bring to a boil over medium heat, without stirring. Add toasted nuts. Reduce heat to low and stir with a wooden spoon for 2 to 4 minutes or until nuts are completely coated and liquid is absorbed.

4. Immediately transfer pecans to bowl containing reserved spice mixture and toss until evenly coated. Spread onto the baking sheet and let cool completely. Transfer to an airtight container, adding any spice mixture that may remain on the baking sheet.

Variation
Substitute walnuts for the pecans.

Olive Spread

1 ½ tbsp	olive oil	22 mL
2	cloves garlic, minced (about 2 tsp/10 mL)	2
1 tbsp	fresh Italian parsley, finely chopped	15 mL
¾ tsp	finely grated lemon zest	3 mL
½ tsp	dried thyme leaves (or 1 ½ tsp/7 mL fresh)	2 mL
¾ cup	pitted dry-cured black olives, finely chopped	175 mL
¼ tsp	freshly ground black pepper	1 mL

Tips

Dry-cured black olives are often heavily salted, although the salt content varies from brand to brand and even between batches of the same brand. If you're trying to restrict your salt intake, use a brand of canned black olives that contains less salt.

This spread is very strong in flavor, so a little goes a long way. It keeps well in the refrigerator for up to 1 week.

1. In a small skillet, heat olive oil with garlic over low heat. Cook for about 30 seconds or until garlic is soft and fragrant but not browned. Remove from heat and stir in parsley, lemon zest and thyme. Transfer to a small bowl, scraping the pan with a spatula to capture all the flavorings.

2. Add olives and pepper to bowl and stir well. Cover and refrigerate for at least 2 hours to allow the flavors to develop.

Variation

To use this spread in a pasta sauce, combine ¼ cup (50 mL) Olive Spread; ¼ cup (50 mL) olive oil; 4 plum tomatoes, seeded and chopped; and ¼ cup (50 mL) finely chopped fresh Italian parsley. Mix well, then toss with 4 cups (1 L) cooked pasta.

Zesty Tofu Spread

Tip

Seasoned salt, commonly found in the spice section of supermarkets, is a blend of different spices, such as paprika, turmeric, onion and garlic. You can substitute garlic or onion salt or, if you prefer, use ¼ tsp (1 mL) table or fine sea salt mixed with minced garlic to taste.

🌿 *Food processor or blender*

6 oz	extra-firm or firm tofu, cut into 1-inch (2.5 cm) cubes	175 g
2 tbsp	olive oil	25 mL
3 tbsp	finely chopped shallot	45 mL
1 tbsp	coarsely chopped fresh Italian parsley	15 mL
1 tbsp	coarsely chopped fresh dillweed (or 1 tsp/5 mL dried)	15 mL
2 tsp	capers, with brine	10 mL
½ tsp	hot pepper sauce	2 mL
¼ tsp	seasoned salt	1 mL

1. On a plate lined with a double layer of paper towels, arrange tofu cubes. Cover with another paper towel and then another plate, and place a weight, such as a large can, on top of the plate to press water out of the tofu. Let drain for 10 minutes. Pour off water and set tofu aside.

2. Meanwhile, in a small skillet, heat olive oil over medium heat for 30 seconds. Add shallot and cook, stirring, for 3 minutes or until softened but not browned. Transfer to food processor or blender. Add parsley, dillweed, capers, hot pepper sauce and seasoned salt and process for 1 minute or until smooth. Add reserved tofu and blend until smooth.

3. Transfer to a bowl, cover and refrigerate for up to 4 days.

> ### Variations
>
> Add 1 tsp (5 mL) flavored or grainy mustard along with the herbs.
>
> If you like bitter flavors, add 1 tsp (5 mL) prepared horseradish or ¼ tsp (1 mL) wasabi powder along with the parsley.
>
> If you don't have capers on hand, use an equal amount of minced dill pickle instead.

Soups

This easy-to-make chowder is tasty and colorful. The earthiness of cumin and the heat of hot pepper flakes complement the natural sweetness of the sweet potato and corn. It is a satisfying meal in itself, but if you want something more substantial, have it with a salad.

Tips

When a liquid is at a simmer, you should see only slight movement on the surface.

Refrigerate this soup in a covered container for up to 3 days. The flavors meld and improve after resting for a day.

Corn and Sweet Potato Chowder

2 tbsp	vegetable oil	25 mL
1	medium onion, finely diced	1
2	cloves garlic, minced (about 2 tsp/10 mL)	2
1	medium sweet potato, peeled and cut into $\frac{1}{2}$-inch (1 cm) cubes	1
1 lb	frozen corn kernels, thawed	500 g
$\frac{1}{4}$ tsp	ground cumin	1 mL
$\frac{1}{4}$ tsp	chili powder	1 mL
4 cups	plain rice or soy milk	1 L
$\frac{1}{2}$ cup	dry mashed potato flakes (instant mashed potatoes)	125 mL
	Salt	

1. In a large pot, heat oil over medium heat for 30 seconds. Add onion and cook, stirring, for 3 minutes or until softened. Add garlic and sweet potato and cook, stirring, for 1 minute. Stir in corn with juices, cumin and chili powder.

2. Increase heat to medium–high. Add rice milk and bring to a boil, stirring occasionally. Place a lid on the pot, leaving 1 inch (2.5 cm) of space between the lid and the rim so the pot is only partially covered. Reduce heat to low and simmer for 12 minutes or until sweet potatoes are soft.

3. Sprinkle with potato flakes and whisk for 1 to 2 minutes or until mixture is thick and smooth. Season with salt to taste.

Variations

For a spicier version, add $\frac{1}{2}$ tsp (2 mL) hot pepper flakes along with the chili powder. To add a tropical twist, finish with a squeeze of lime juice and a garnish of finely chopped fresh cilantro leaves.

Garnish each serving with 1 tsp (5 mL) each of finely chopped green onion and fresh parsley.

Lentil Soup

Tips

Unlike dried beans, lentils do not need to be soaked before cooking. They do, however, need to be thoroughly rinsed and inspected for bits of dirt and other impurities. We recommend submerging lentils completely in water, then picking out any impurities that float to the top. Drain in a colander, remove any remaining impurities or blackened lentils and rinse thoroughly under cold running water before using in a recipe.

Onion stock is available in many supermarkets and natural food stores. If you don't have it on hand, replace it with an equal amount of vegetable stock and add an additional half an onion, finely chopped, in Step 1. The vegetable stock will absorb the flavor of the onion quite well.

1 ½ tbsp	olive oil	22 mL
1	large onion, finely chopped	1
½ cup	finely chopped celery	125 mL
2	carrots, peeled and thinly sliced	2
3	cloves garlic, minced (about 1 tbsp/15 mL)	3
4 cups	vegetable stock	1 L
3 cups	onion stock (see Tips, left)	750 mL
1	can (14 oz/398 mL) diced tomatoes, with juices	1
1 cup	brown lentils, washed, rinsed and drained (see Tips, left)	250 mL
2 tsp	white wine vinegar	10 mL
	Salt and freshly ground black pepper	

1. In a large pot, heat oil over medium heat for 30 seconds. Add onion, celery and carrots and cook, stirring, for 4 minutes or until softened, adding a little water and reducing heat to medium-low if vegetables start to brown. Add garlic and cook, stirring, for 1 minute.

2. Add vegetable stock, onion stock, tomatoes, lentils and vinegar and bring to a boil. Reduce heat to low and simmer, uncovered, for 30 to 35 minutes or until lentils are soft and flavor develops. Season with salt and pepper to taste.

Variations

To add texture and flavor, add 1 tsp (5 mL) dried basil leaves along with the vegetable stock, and 1 cup (250 mL) chopped fresh spinach leaves or kale after the lentils have cooked for 15 to 20 minutes.

For a more substantial main course, place ½ cup (125 mL) warm cooked rice in a soup bowl and add 1 cup (250 mL) Lentil Soup.

Here's a thick, chunky and tasty soup the whole family can enjoy.

Tips

Beans are a nutritious alternative to meat and are high in iron and folate.

Because can sizes vary, we provide a range of amounts for beans in our recipes. If you're using 19-oz (540 mL) cans, add an additional 2 cups (500 mL) vegetable stock, 2 tsp (10 mL) red wine vinegar and a pinch more dried basil and chili powder.

If you prefer a smoother soup, purée the tomatoes in a food processor or blender before adding to soup in Step 2.

Hearty Black and White Bean Soup

Food processor or blender

1½ tbsp	olive oil	22 mL
1	large onion, finely chopped	1
3	cloves garlic, minced (about 1 tbsp/15 mL)	3
2	medium carrots, peeled and thinly sliced	2
2	stalks celery, coarsely chopped	2
4 cups	vegetable stock	1 L
1	can (28 oz/796 mL) diced tomatoes, with juices	1
2	cans (each 14 to 19 oz/398 to 540 mL) black beans, drained and rinsed, or 2 cups (500 mL) dried black beans, soaked, cooked and drained (see Legumes, page 13)	2
1	can (14 to 19 oz/398 to 540 mL) white beans, drained and rinsed, or 1 cup (250 mL) dried white beans, soaked, cooked and drained (see Legumes, page 13)	1
2 tbsp	red wine vinegar	25 mL
1½ tbsp	chili powder	22 mL
1 tbsp	dried basil leaves	15 mL
	Salt and freshly ground black pepper	

1. In a large pot, heat oil over medium heat for 30 seconds. Add onion and garlic and cook, stirring, for 3 minutes or until softened. Add carrots and celery and cook, stirring, for 3 minutes.

2. Stir in vegetable stock and tomatoes and bring to a boil. Reduce heat to medium-low and cook, uncovered, for 10 minutes or until vegetables are tender.

3. Meanwhile, in food processor or blender, process half of the black beans to achieve a thick pastelike consistency. Stir into soup. Add the remaining black beans and white beans.

4. Add red wine vinegar, chili powder, basil, salt and pepper to taste. Stir well. Reduce heat to low, cover and simmer for 15 minutes or until the flavors meld.

Variations

Purée the entire soup to completely blend flavors. This will give you a thick, rich result.

Add two sliced smoked soy sausages, thawed if frozen, after the soup has finished cooking. Cook for 5 minutes longer or until sausages are heated through. Garnish with chopped fresh basil or cilantro leaves, to taste.

For a more filling meal, spoon ½ cup (125 mL) hot cooked pasta or rice into each soup bowl. Add 1 cup (250 mL) of the hot soup, stir and serve. Accompany with Italian or herbed bread, if desired.

*Udon noodles are a staple
in Japanese cuisine. These
soft, doughy noodles are
now available in many
supermarkets and specialty
stores. Both kids and adults
love them because they are
fun to eat.*

Tips

In many locations, green
onions are known as
scallions.

Some udon noodles come
precooked. If you are using
this type, remove the soup
from the heat once it
comes back to a boil.

Hot-and-Sour Udon Noodle Soup

6 cups	vegetable stock	1.5 L
1⅓ cups	snow peas, ends trimmed and cut into 1-inch (2.5 cm) pieces	325 mL
1 cup	chopped bok choy	250 mL
3	green onions (white and green parts), coarsely chopped (see Tips, left)	3
¼ cup	low-sodium soy sauce	50 mL
¼ cup	seasoned rice vinegar	50 mL
2½ tsp	sesame oil	12 mL
	Freshly ground black pepper	
1 lb	udon noodles (see Tips, left)	500 g
	Hot chili oil	

1. In a large pot, combine vegetable stock, snow peas, bok choy, green onions, soy sauce, vinegar, sesame oil and black pepper to taste. Bring to a boil over medium–high heat. Reduce heat to low and cook, uncovered, for 5 minutes or until vegetables are tender.

2. Add noodles. Increase heat to medium and bring to a boil. Reduce heat to low and simmer, uncovered, for 5 minutes or until noodles are tender. Season with chili oil to taste.

Variation

For a heartier, more complex soup, add broccoli florets, baby corn, bamboo shoots, water chestnuts or 1-inch (2.5 cm) cubes of tofu. Add along with the bok choy.

This soup is delicious at any temperature: hot, cold or room temperature. Served in smaller portions, it makes an appetizing first course.

Tip

If you are not using an immersion blender and time permits, allow the soup to cool before puréeing. Use caution as you blend hot soup, particularly if using a blender. Fill the blender container only half-full to avoid the build up of steam, which can cause the lid to pop off.

Curried Carrot and Pear Soup

Food processor or blender

2 tbsp	vegetable oil	25 mL
1	medium onion, thinly sliced	1
1 tbsp	curry powder	15 mL
2	cloves garlic, minced (about 2 tsp/10 mL)	2
8 cups	vegetable stock	2 L
4	large carrots, coarsely chopped	4
2	pears, peeled, cored and sliced, divided	2
1 tbsp	packed light brown sugar or other dry sweetener	15 mL
3 tbsp	freshly squeezed lemon juice, divided	45 mL
	Salt and freshly ground black pepper	

1. In a large pot, heat oil over medium heat for 30 seconds. Add onion and cook, stirring, for 3 minutes or until softened. Add curry powder and garlic and cook, stirring, for 1 minute or until fragrant.

2. Add vegetable stock, carrots, all but one-quarter of one pear, and sugar and bring to a boil. Reduce heat and simmer, uncovered, for 20 minutes or until carrots are soft and soup is fragrant.

3. In a food processor or blender, or using an immersion blender, purée soup, in batches if necessary, until smooth (see Tip, left). If necessary, return to pot and reheat until steaming.

4. Add 2 tbsp (25 mL) lemon juice and season with salt and pepper to taste. Grate remaining pear and drizzle with remaining lemon juice to keep from browning. Ladle soup into cups or bowls and top with grated pear mixture.

Variation

If you enjoy a bit of spice, add an extra 2 tsp (10 mL) curry powder, 1 tsp (5 mL) grated gingerroot and pinch hot pepper flakes along with the curry powder.

Minestrone

There is very little that you can do wrong with this nourishing soup. Full of vitamins and minerals, it is hearty enough to enjoy as a meal, and it tastes great as a leftover.

Tips

When cooking potatoes and pasta in a broth, be aware that they tend to absorb a lot of the liquid. If the soup is becoming too thick, add a little water or vegetable stock. If you have leftovers, you may find that the vegetables soak up the liquid during storage. Just add more liquid when reheating.

You can find natural cane sugar in the baking section of natural food stores and many supermarkets.

2 tbsp	olive oil	25 mL
1	large onion, finely chopped	1
3	cloves garlic, minced (about 1 tbsp/15 mL)	3
2	stalks celery, finely chopped	2
2	medium carrots, peeled and thinly sliced	2
6 cups	vegetable stock	1.5 L
1	large potato, peeled and cut into 3/4-inch (2 cm) cubes	1
3/4 cup	ditalini or other small tube-shaped pasta	175 mL
1	can (14 to 19 oz/398 to 540 mL) red kidney beans, drained and rinsed, or 1 cup (250 mL) dried red kidney beans, soaked, cooked and drained (see Legumes, page 13)	1
1	can (14 oz/398 mL) whole tomatoes, with juices	1
2 tbsp	tomato paste	25 mL
2 tsp	red wine vinegar	10 mL
2 tbsp	coarsely chopped fresh basil leaves (or 2 tsp/10 mL dried)	25 mL
2 tbsp	natural cane sugar (approx), see Tips, left	25 mL
1 tbsp	coarsely chopped fresh oregano leaves (or 1 tsp/5 mL dried)	15 mL
	Salt and freshly ground black pepper	

1. In a large pot, heat oil over medium heat for 30 seconds. Add onion and cook, stirring, for 3 minutes or until softened. Add garlic, celery and carrots and cook, stirring, for 3 to 4 minutes. Increase heat to medium–high. Add vegetable stock, potato, pasta and kidney beans and bring to a boil. Reduce heat to medium and cook, uncovered, for 10 minutes or until potato is tender.

2. In a blender or food processor, purée tomatoes with juices until smooth. Add tomato paste and red wine vinegar and pulse to blend. Stir tomato mixture into soup.

3. Reduce heat to low and stir in basil, sugar, oregano and salt and pepper to taste. Cook, uncovered, for 10 minutes or until pasta is tender.

Variations

Add 1 cup (250 mL) chopped fresh green beans along with the stock.

For a heartier soup, add a can of chickpeas and an additional 1 cup (250 mL) vegetable stock along with the puréed tomatoes.

For a flavorful finish, garnish each serving with 1 tbsp (15 mL) chopped fresh parsley.

Leek and Potato Soup

This classic French soup works well cold or hot. Plain rice milk in the base allows the potato and leek flavors to fully develop their rich subtlety.

Tips

To make the bouquet garni for this recipe, wrap three sprigs fresh thyme or ½ tsp (2 mL) dried thyme leaves, four parsley stems, and one bay leaf in a square of cheesecloth (see page 17 for more information on bouquets garnis).

Leeks are usually quite gritty. To clean, cut off the root end and the darkest green parts. With a sharp knife, split leeks open lengthwise and cut each half in half again to make four sections. Slice to the required size and drop into a large bowl of cold water. Swish around, then lift leeks out of water with your hands or a slotted spoon. The grit will collect at the bottom of the bowl. Repeat, using a fresh bowl of water if any sign of dirt still remains.

For salt-restricted diets, use only a portion of the salt called for in the recipe and offer additional salt at the table for those who want it.

If you are not using an immersion blender and time permits, allow the soup to cool before puréeing (see Tip, page 52).

✎ Food processor or blender

2 tbsp	vegetable oil	25 mL
3	leeks (white and light green parts only), washed and thinly sliced (see Tips, left)	3
2 tsp	salt, divided (see Tips, left)	10 mL
1	large baking potato, peeled and coarsely chopped	1
1	bouquet garni (see Tips, left)	1
4 cups	plain rice milk	1 L
3 cups	water	750 mL
Pinch	cayenne pepper or ground white pepper	Pinch
1½ tbsp	lemon juice, divided	22 mL
2 tsp	chopped fresh chives or green onions	10 mL
Pinch	finely chopped fresh Italian parsley, optional	Pinch

1. In a pot, heat vegetable oil over medium heat for 30 seconds. Add leeks and cook, stirring, for 3 minutes or until slightly softened. Sprinkle leeks with 1 tsp (5 mL) salt and continue to cook for another 3 to 4 minutes or until soft but not browned.

2. Add potato, bouquet garni, rice milk, water and cayenne pepper. Increase heat to high and bring to a boil. Reduce heat to low and simmer, uncovered, for 15 to 20 minutes or until potatoes are tender. Stir in half of the lemon juice. Discard bouquet garni.

3. In a food processor or blender, or using an immersion blender, purée soup, in batches if necessary, until smooth. If necessary, return soup to pot and reheat until steaming if serving hot.

4. Add remaining lemon juice. Mix well and season with remaining salt to taste. Stir in chives, and Italian parsley, if using. Serve hot or cold. If serving cold, cover and refrigerate for 2 to 3 hours or until chilled.

This classic soup, with a base of dark roasted-vegetable stock and caramelized onions, is a soul-satisfying favorite for family and friends.

Tips

If you can't find roasted vegetable stock, use regular vegetable stock.

Leftover portions of this soup can be used as a sauce for pasta and grain dishes. It can also be thickened and used as a sauce for a stir-fry of vegetables and tofu. To thicken soup, make a roux by whisking 1 tbsp (15 mL) margarine with 1 tbsp (15 mL) all-purpose flour in a small pot over medium heat for 30 seconds. Whisk in 1 cup (250 mL) soup, ¼ cup (50 mL) at a time, mixing well after each addition. Bring to a boil and cook, stirring, until thickened.

Onion Soup with Crostini

❧ *Preheat oven to 400°F (200°C)*
❧ *Large baking sheet, ungreased*

¼ cup	soy margarine	50 mL
2 lbs	onions, thinly sliced (about 6 medium)	1 kg
1 tbsp	granulated natural cane sugar or other dry sweetener	15 mL
½ tsp	minced garlic	2 mL
½ cup	all-purpose flour	125 mL
8 cups	roasted vegetable stock (see Tips, left)	2 L
⅓ cup	dry sherry or dry white wine	75 mL
2 tsp	dried thyme leaves	10 mL
1 tsp	salt, or to taste	5 mL
¼ tsp	freshly ground black pepper	1 mL
CROSTINI		
2 tbsp	olive oil	25 mL
½ tsp	minced garlic	2 mL
6 to 8	½-inch (1 cm) thick slices French bread	6 to 8
1 tbsp	chopped fresh Italian parsley, optional	15 mL

1. In a large pot, melt margarine over medium heat. Stir in onions and sugar and cook, stirring often, for 20 minutes or until onions turn limp and light brown. Add garlic and cook, stirring, for 30 seconds. Sprinkle flour over onion mixture and cook, stirring with a wooden spoon to prevent scorching, for 1 minute.

2. Gradually add stock, whisking constantly to prevent lumps from forming. Add sherry, thyme, salt and pepper and bring to a boil. Reduce heat to low and simmer, partially covered, for 25 minutes.

3. *Crostini:* In a small bowl, mix olive oil with garlic. Lightly brush both sides of bread with garlic oil. Place on baking sheet and toast in preheated oven, turning once, for 10 minutes or until golden, crisp and fragrant.

4. Ladle soup into bowls and float one crostini on top. Sprinkle with parsley, if using.

Fresh Minted Pea Soup

Food processor or blender

This soup, which is a warm-weather version of the hearty dried split pea soup, can be puréed using a blender or left in a chunkier form with flecks of orange carrot dotting the surface. It is especially delicious served cold.

Tips

Bouquet garni is a French term for a bundle of seasonings that are usually wrapped in cheesecloth and tied with kitchen string. For this recipe, we use three sprigs of fresh thyme or 1/2 tsp (2 mL) dried thyme leaves, four parsley stems and one bay leaf.

If you are not using an immersion blender and time permits, allow the soup to cool before puréeing. Use caution as you blend hot soup, particularly if using a blender. Fill the blender container only half-full to avoid the buildup of steam, which can cause the lid to pop off.

3 tbsp	vegetable oil	45 mL
2	leeks, washed and thinly sliced (about 3 cups/750 mL), see Tips, page 50	2
2	shallots, finely chopped (about 3 tbsp/45 mL)	2
2	carrots, peeled and chopped	2
1 lb	frozen green peas	500 mL
3 cups	vegetable stock	750 mL
3 cups	plain rice milk or soy milk	750 mL
1	bouquet garni (see Tips, left)	
1 tsp	dried mint leaves (or 1 tbsp/15 mL chopped fresh)	5 mL
1/4 cup	coarsely chopped fresh Italian parsley	50 mL
2 tbsp	freshly squeezed lemon juice	25 mL
1/2 tsp	granulated natural cane sugar, optional	2 mL
	Salt and freshly ground black pepper	

1. In a large pot, heat oil over medium heat for 30 seconds. Add leeks and cook, stirring, for 3 minutes or until softened. Add shallots and carrots and cook, stirring, for 3 minutes or until fragrant.

2. Stir in peas, vegetable stock, rice milk, bouquet garni and mint and bring to a boil. Reduce heat and simmer, uncovered, for 10 minutes or until peas are tender and flavor develops. Discard bouquet garni. Add parsley and let stand for 1 minute.

3. In a food processor or blender, or using an immersion blender (see Tips, left), purée soup, in batches if necessary, until smooth or desired texture is achieved. If necessary, return soup to pot and reheat until steaming.

4. Stir in lemon juice, and sugar, if using. Season with salt and pepper to taste. Serve hot. If you prefer a cold soup, transfer to a bowl, cover and refrigerate for 2 to 3 hours or until thoroughly chilled.

Variations

A chiffonade of lettuce leaves and fresh mint leaves makes a nice garnish for this soup. To make a chiffonade, use a soft lettuce such as Boston, Bibb or leaf. Make a tight roll of a lettuce leaf and another of two or three mint leaves. Thinly slice each roll into ⅛-inch (0.25 cm) thick strips. You will have thin ribbons, which are delicate and light enough to float on the soup, making an attractive topping.

Another topping, drawn from Indian flavors, can be made with a dollop of puréed silken tofu mixed with 1 tsp (5 mL) finely minced crystallized ginger and a splash of mint vinegar. It makes a refreshing contrast in flavors and textures.

Tomato Soup

Tips

In many locations, green onions are known as scallions.

If you prefer a smoother soup, purée in batches until the desired consistency is achieved.

2 tbsp	olive oil	25 mL
1	large onion, coarsely chopped	1
4	cloves garlic, minced (about 4 tsp/20 mL)	4
1 cup	baby carrots, cut into thirds	250 mL
2	stalks celery, coarsely chopped	2
4 cups	vegetable stock	1 L
1	can (28 oz/796 mL) diced tomatoes, with juices	1
2 tsp	dried basil leaves	10 mL
2 tsp	red wine vinegar	10 mL
1/2 tsp	salt, or to taste	2 mL
1/2 tsp	freshly ground black pepper, or to taste	2 mL
1	bunch green onions (green and white parts), coarsely chopped (1 cup/250 mL), see Tips, left	1

1. In a large pot, heat oil over medium heat for 30 seconds. Add onion and cook, stirring, for 3 minutes or until softened. Add garlic and cook, stirring, for 1 minute. Stir in carrots and celery. Reduce heat to low, cover and cook for 12 to 15 minutes or until vegetables are softened.

2. Stir in vegetable stock, diced tomatoes with juices, basil and vinegar and bring to a boil. Reduce heat and simmer, uncovered, for 10 minutes or until flavors meld.

3. Stir in salt, pepper and green onions and simmer, uncovered, for 30 minutes or until soup reaches desired thickness.

Variations

Tomato Rice Soup: In each serving bowl, combine 1/2 cup (125 mL) warm cooked rice and 1 cup (250 mL) hot Tomato Soup.

Cream of Tomato Soup: Add 1/2 to 3/4 cup (125 to 175 mL) plain or vanilla-flavor soy milk along with the green onions.

Spicy Tomato Soup: Add hot pepper sauce to taste along with the salt and pepper.

Rosemary Tomato Soup: Add 1 tbsp (15 mL) dried rosemary leaves along with the garlic.

Tomato Soup with Fennel: Add 1 tbsp (15 mL) fennel seeds along with the garlic.

Mushroom and Barley Soup

This hearty comfort food is perfect on a cold winter's night. For a particularly satisfying meal, serve this with a zesty, bold salad, such as Caesar Salad with Capers (see recipe, page 67).

Tips

You can often find mushroom stock in your supermarket or natural foods store. If you can't find it, use vegetable stock instead and add an additional 4 oz (125 g) sliced mushrooms along with the 8 oz (250 g) called for in the recipe.

Choose canned diced tomatoes with or without seasonings for this soup.

2 tbsp	vegetable or olive oil	25 mL
1	large onion, finely chopped	1
4	cloves garlic, minced (about 1 1/2 tbsp/22 mL)	4
2	carrots, peeled and thinly sliced	2
1	stalk celery, finely chopped	1
8 oz	mushrooms, thinly sliced	250 g
4 cups	mushroom stock (see Tips, left)	1 L
4 cups	vegetable stock	1 L
1	can (14 oz/398 mL) diced tomatoes, with juices	1
1 cup	pearl barley, rinsed and drained	250 mL
2 tsp	dried thyme leaves	10 mL
1 tsp	white wine vinegar	5 mL
1/4 tsp	freshly ground black pepper, or to taste	1 mL
1	bay leaf	1
	Salt	

1. In a large pot, heat oil over medium heat for 30 seconds. Add onion and cook, stirring, for 3 minutes or until softened. Add garlic, carrots, celery and mushrooms and cook, stirring frequently, for 7 minutes or until mushrooms start to brown.

2. Add mushroom and vegetable stocks, tomatoes, barley, thyme, vinegar, pepper, bay leaf and salt to taste. Stir well and bring to a boil. Reduce heat to medium–low and simmer, uncovered, for 30 minutes or until barley is tender. Remove bay leaf before serving.

Variations

Replace thyme with half the amount of dried rosemary leaves.

If you like spice, add hot pepper sauce to taste before serving.

This deeply flavorful soup delivers a rich, creamy texture. Serve this as a main course accompanied by bread and salad.

Tips

You'll need about 1 tbsp (15 mL) coarsely chopped garlic and 2 lbs (1 kg) butternut squash to make this soup.

You can often find mushroom stock with the stocks and bouillons in your supermarket or natural foods store. If you can't find it, use vegetable stock instead and add 4 oz (125 g) sliced mushrooms.

If you are not using an immersion blender and time permits, allow the soup to cool before puréeing. Use caution as you blend hot soup, particularly if using a blender. Fill the blender container only half-full to avoid the buildup of steam, which can cause the lid to pop off.

Spicy Squash and Fennel Soup

❧ Food processor or blender

2 tbsp	olive oil (approx)	25 mL
1	large onion, finely chopped	1
3	cloves garlic, coarsely chopped	3
1 tbsp	all-purpose flour	15 mL
4 cups	mushroom stock (see Tip, left)	1 L
4 cups	vegetable stock	1 L
1	butternut squash, peeled and cut into 1-inch (2.5 cm) cubes	1
Half	head Chinese cabbage, coarsely chopped (about 4 cups/1 L)	Half
Half	bulb fennel coarsely chopped	Half
1 1/4 tsp	ground cumin	6 mL
1 tsp	mustard seeds	5 mL
1/2 tsp	fennel seeds	2 mL
	Hot pepper flakes	
	Salt and freshly ground black pepper	

1. In a large saucepan, heat oil over medium heat for 30 seconds. Add onion and cook, stirring, for 3 minutes or until softened. Add garlic and cook, stirring, for 1 minute. Add flour and cook, stirring, for 1 minute, adding more oil if necessary to make a stiff, doughy texture.

2. Gradually whisk in mushroom and vegetable stocks and bring to a boil. Add squash, Chinese cabbage and fennel bulb and simmer, uncovered, for 20 minutes or until vegetables are tender.

3. Stir in cumin, mustard seeds, fennel seeds and hot pepper flakes, salt and freshly ground black pepper to taste. Cook for 10 minutes or until flavor is developed. Remove from heat and let cool for 10 minutes.

4. In a food processor or blender, or using an immersion blender (see Tips, left), purée soup, in batches if necessary, until smooth or desired texture is achieved. If necessary, return soup to pot and reheat until steaming.

Variation

For those who have more adventurous palates, pass hot pepper sauce at the table.

This cool, refreshing soup is one of the most appropriate dishes to celebrate summer. This rendition can be enjoyed year-round with readily available ingredients.

Tips

In many locations, green onions are known as scallions.

Cutting the vegetables by hand is one secret of good gazpacho. Over the years we have come to prefer larger diced vegetables to those that are finely diced, because they share their distinct textures and tastes much better.

Gazpacho doesn't keep for longer than a few days. It is at its peak a few hours after it is made. As with all chilled dishes, it may require additional seasoning before serving to make up for the blunting effect of cold on the palate.

Gazpacho

4 cups	tomato or vegetable juice	1 L
1	can (28 oz/796 mL) diced tomatoes, with juices, or 3 cups (750 mL) diced seeded fresh tomatoes	1
2	cloves garlic, minced (about 2 tsp/10 mL)	2
1	cucumber, peeled	1
3	stalks celery	3
Half	sweet or red onion, diced	Half
1	green bell pepper, seeded and cut into $1/2$-inch (1 cm) cubes	1
4	green onions (white and light green parts only), thinly sliced (see Tips, left)	4
3 tbsp	red wine vinegar	45 mL
1 tsp	granulated natural cane sugar or other dry sweetener	5 mL
	Salt and freshly ground black pepper	
$1\frac{1}{2}$ tbsp	olive oil	22 mL

1. In a large bowl, combine tomato juice, diced tomatoes and garlic. Set aside.

2. Cut cucumber lengthwise into quarters. Cut each quarter lengthwise, into two thin pieces. Cut pieces crosswise into $1/8$-inch (0.25 cm) thick slices. Stir into tomato mixture.

3. Cut celery stalks in half lengthwise to make long narrow strips. Cut strips crosswise into $1/8$-inch (0.25 cm) thick slices. Stir into tomato mixture. Add onion, pepper and green onions and stir well.

4. In a small bowl, whisk together vinegar, sugar and salt and pepper to taste. Add olive oil and mix well. Stir into tomato mixture. Cover and refrigerate for at least 2 hours to allow soup to develop its full flavor or for up to 3 days. Serve chilled.

Variations

This soup takes on different flavors with the addition of fresh summer herbs, such as dill, tarragon, basil or chives, each of which gives it a distinctly different personality.

Cubes of avocado can also be added to make it more substantial, and diced orange and yellow bell peppers add color. Thin slices of cucumber or toasted croutons make a nice garnish.

This is a crowd-pleaser, and it's equally delicious served hot or cold. It makes a refreshing summer lunch or a light dinner served with salad and bread.

Tips

If you prefer, substitute fresh gingerroot for the ground ginger. Use a 2- by 1-inch (5 by 2.5 cm) piece, peeled and finely grated.

If you are not using an immersion blender and time permits, allow the soup to cool before puréeing. Use caution as you blend hot soup, particularly if using a blender. Fill the blender container only half-full to avoid the buildup of steam, which can cause the lid to pop off.

Butternut Squash and Apple Soup with Ginger

➤ Preheat oven to 450°F (230°C)
➤ Baking sheet, greased
➤ Food processor or blender

1	butternut squash, unpeeled (about 2 lbs/1 kg)	1
2 tbsp	vegetable oil	25 mL
1	onion, coarsely chopped	1
2	tart apples, such as Granny Smith, cored, peeled and coarsely chopped	2
2	cloves garlic, thinly sliced (about 2 tsp/10 mL)	2
5 cups	water	1.25 L
3 cups	apple cider	750 mL
1 tsp	ground ginger (see Tips, left)	5 mL
Pinch	cayenne pepper	Pinch
	Salt and freshly ground black pepper	
	Hot pepper sauce, optional	

1. Cut squash in half lengthwise. Scrape out seeds with a spoon. On prepared pan, place squash, cut side down. Bake for 30 to 40 minutes or until soft.

2. Meanwhile, in a large pot, heat oil over medium heat for 30 seconds. Add onion and cook, stirring, for 3 minutes or until softened. Add apples and garlic and cook, stirring, for 2 to 3 minutes or until apples are softened but not browned. Stir in water, cider, ginger and cayenne pepper and bring to a boil. Reduce heat to medium-low and simmer, uncovered, for 25 minutes or until flavors develop.

3. Using a large spoon, scoop cooked squash out of skin and add to pot, discarding skin. Increase heat to medium and simmer for 5 minutes longer.

4. In a food processor or blender, or using an immersion blender, purée soup, in batches if necessary, until smooth. If necessary, return soup to pot and reheat until steaming. Season to taste with salt, pepper and hot pepper sauce, if using.

Variation

Garnish with thin slices of apple with skin, cut into thin sticks. Place on top of each serving and sprinkle with freshly cracked black peppercorns.

Curried Potato and Chickpea Soup

Tips

If potatoes and carrots stick to the pot, try adding 1 to 2 tbsp (15 to 25 mL) water while softening.

Because can sizes vary, we provide a range of amounts for beans in our recipes. If you're using the larger size, you may want to adjust the seasoning by adding an additional pinch of curry powder, cumin and sugar to suit your taste.

2 tbsp	olive oil	25 mL
1	onion, finely chopped	1
1 tbsp	curry powder	15 mL
1 tbsp	ground cumin	15 mL
2	potatoes, peeled and cut into ¾-inch (2 cm) cubes	2
2	carrots, peeled and thinly sliced	2
4 cups	vegetable stock	1 L
1	can (14 to 19 oz/398 to 540 mL) chickpeas, drained and rinsed (see Tips, left)	1
1	can (14 oz/398 mL) coconut milk	1
½ cup	vanilla-flavor soy milk	125 mL
1	can (14 oz/398 mL) crushed tomatoes	1
2 tsp	granulated natural cane sugar	10 mL
	Salt and freshly ground black pepper	

1. In a large pot, heat oil over medium heat for 30 seconds. Add onion and cook, stirring, for 3 minutes or until softened. Add curry powder and cumin and cook, stirring, for 1 minute. Reduce heat to low and add potatoes and carrots. Cook, stirring, for 3 minutes or until vegetables begin to soften (see Tips, left).

2. Add vegetable stock, chickpeas, coconut milk, soy milk and tomatoes. Increase heat to medium–high and bring to a boil. Reduce heat to low and simmer, uncovered, for 10 minutes or until vegetables are soft.

3. Add sugar and salt and pepper to taste. Simmer, uncovered, for 25 minutes or until flavors develop.

Variation

Add a pinch of cayenne pepper or a dash of hot pepper sauce to taste for a spicier soup. Garnish each serving with a sprig of fresh cilantro or parsley, if desired.

Salads, Sandwiches and Wraps

This salad, which combines the refreshing flavors of tarragon, lemon and garlic, may even be better the day after it is made.

Tips

Unlike dried beans, lentils don't need to be soaked before cooking. You should, however, submerge them in water and remove any impurities that float to the top. Drain in a colander, remove any remaining impurities or blackened lentils and rinse thoroughly under cold running water before using in a recipe.

Cooking times will vary depending upon the kind of lentils you use and how long they have been in storage. Generally, the longer they are stored, the longer they take to cook.

Lentil Salad with Tomatoes and Tarragon

6 cups	water	1.5 L
1 tbsp	salt	15 mL
1 cup	brown or green lentils, washed, rinsed and drained (see Tips, left)	250 mL
½ cup	diced red bell pepper	125 mL
¼ cup	olive oil	50 mL
½ tsp	grated lemon zest	2 mL
2 tbsp	freshly squeezed lemon juice	25 mL
1	clove garlic, minced (about 1 tsp/5 mL)	1
1 tbsp	chopped fresh tarragon, divided (or 1 tsp/5 mL dried, divided)	15 mL
1 tsp	Dijon mustard	5 mL
¼ tsp	freshly ground black pepper	1 mL
1 cup	quartered cherry tomatoes	250 mL
1 tsp	red wine vinegar	5 mL
	Salt, optional	

1. In a large pot, bring water and salt to a boil over high heat. Add lentils and return to a boil. Reduce heat and simmer, uncovered, for 20 to 30 minutes or until lentils are tender but firm. Drain, shaking strainer well to remove excess moisture.

2. In a bowl, whisk together red pepper, olive oil, lemon zest and juice, garlic, 2 tsp (10 mL) tarragon, mustard and black pepper until well blended. Add lentils and toss until evenly coated. Transfer to a serving bowl.

3. In a small bowl, combine tomatoes, remaining 1 tsp (5 mL) tarragon, vinegar and salt to taste, if using. Arrange tomato mixture over lentil mixture or around the edge of the bowl to make a colorful ring.

Variation

In Step 3, replace the tomato mixture with 2 green onions, sliced; 2 stalks celery, thinly sliced; ¼ cup (50 mL) black olives; 1 tbsp (15 mL) chopped parsley; 1 tbsp (15 mL) olive oil; and 2 tsp (10 mL) red wine vinegar. Combine in a small bowl, sprinkle over the lentil mixture and serve.

Black Bean Salad

Black beans are a terrific source of protein, fiber and iron. Enjoy this Mexican-inspired salad over a bed of lettuce.

Tips

Because can sizes vary, we provide a range of amounts for beans in our recipes. If you're using 19–oz (540 mL) cans, add an additional 1 tsp (5 mL) lime juice, ¼ tsp (1 mL) cumin and a pinch of adobo seasoning.

Adobo seasoning is a spice mixture composed of salt, garlic, black pepper, oregano and turmeric. If you can't find it, substitute a pinch each of garlic powder, oregano and turmeric and salt and black pepper to taste.

You can use 1¾ cups (425 mL) frozen corn kernels, thawed and drained, instead of the canned corn. If you prefer to use fresh corn, boil 4 ears of corn for 4 to 5 minutes in lightly salted water. When it is cool enough to handle, slide a knife down the length of the cob to remove kernels. Measure out 1¾ cups (425 mL) kernels.

3 tbsp	olive oil, divided	45 mL
1	red onion, finely chopped (about 1½ cups/375 mL)	1
1	clove garlic, minced (about 1 tsp/5 mL)	1
2	cans (each 14 to 19 oz/398 to 540 mL) black beans, drained and rinsed (see Tips, left), or 2 cups (500 mL) dried black beans, soaked, cooked and drained (see Legumes, page 13)	2
2½ tbsp	freshly squeezed lime juice	32 mL
2 tsp	granulated natural cane sugar, or to taste	10 mL
1 tsp	ground cumin	5 mL
½ tsp	adobo seasoning or Mexican spice blend (see Tips, left)	2 mL
1/4 tsp	hot pepper sauce, or to taste	1 mL
2	cans (each 7 oz/213 mL) corn kernels, drained (see Tips, left)	
2	large tomatoes, seeded and finely diced	2
½ cup	coarsely chopped fresh cilantro leaves	125 mL
	Salt and freshly ground black pepper	

1. In a large skillet, heat 1 tbsp (15 mL) oil over medium heat for 30 seconds. Add onion and cook, stirring, for 3 minutes or until softened. Add garlic and cook, stirring, for 1 minute. Stir in beans and reduce heat to medium-low. Cook for 4 minutes or until beans are heated through.

2. Meanwhile, in a small bowl, whisk together lime juice, sugar, cumin, adobo seasoning, hot pepper sauce and remaining olive oil until well blended.

3. In a serving bowl, combine bean mixture, corn, tomatoes and cilantro. Add dressing and toss until evenly coated. Season with salt and pepper to taste. Cover and refrigerate for 2 hours or until chilled. This salad can be refrigerated in an airtight container for up to 3 days.

Roasted Red Potato Salad

Tip

In many locations, green
onions are known as
scallions.

1	batch Roasted Red Potatoes (see recipe, page 158), cooled to room temperature (3 lbs/1.5 kg)	1
1 cup	diced red bell pepper	250 mL
¼ cup	coarsely chopped green onions (see Tip, left)	50 mL
⅔ cup	soy mayonnaise	150 mL
2 tbsp	vegan sour cream alternative	25 mL
2 tbsp	Dijon mustard	25 mL
1 tbsp	cider vinegar	15 mL
1 tbsp	granulated natural cane sugar, or to taste	15 mL

1. In a large bowl, combine potatoes, red pepper and green onions. Mix well. Set aside.

2. In a small bowl, whisk together soy mayonnaise, vegan sour cream, mustard, vinegar and sugar. Add to potato mixture and toss to coat evenly. Cover and refrigerate for at least 3 hours or until chilled. This salad is best eaten within 3 days.

Soy Bacon, Basil and Tomato
Sandwich *(see variation, page 77)*

Overleaf: Hot-and-Sour Udon
Noodle Soup *(page 46)*

Four-Bean Salad

This fresh and zesty salad is a great accompaniment to almost any meal. Serve with crusty whole wheat bread to soak up the tasty vinaigrette.

Tips

Because can sizes vary, we provide a range of amounts for beans in our recipes. If you're using 19–oz (540 mL) cans, make the dressing using 1 cup (250 mL) cider vinegar, ½ cup (125 mL) vegetable oil, 4 cloves garlic, 1 tbsp (15 mL) fresh basil and 1½ tsp (7 mL) tarragon.

Use soaked, cooked and drained dried beans rather than canned, if you prefer. (See Legumes, page 13, for cooking instructions.)

When steaming vegetables, make sure that the bottom of the steamer does not touch the water — otherwise they will boil, not steam. Add just enough water to the pot to create steam yet keep the vegetables above water.

Spaghetti and Soyballs
(page 80)

꙰ Steamer

DRESSING

⅔ cup	cider vinegar	150 mL
⅓ cup	vegetable oil	75 mL
3	cloves garlic, minced (about 1 tbsp/15 mL)	3
2 tsp	chopped fresh basil leaves (or 1 tsp/5 mL dried)	10 mL
1 tsp	dried tarragon leaves	5 mL
	Salt and freshly ground black pepper	

SALAD

3 cups	chopped trimmed green beans (1-inch/2.5 cm pieces)	750 mL
1	can (14 to 19 oz/398 to 540 mL) red kidney beans, drained and rinsed (see Tips, left)	1
1	can (14 to 19 oz/398 to 540 mL) white kidney beans, drained and rinsed	1
1	can (14 to 19 oz/398 to 540 mL) chickpeas, drained and rinsed	1
1	red bell pepper, diced	1
1	red onion, cut in half from root to stem and thinly sliced on the vertical	1

1. *Dressing:* In a bowl, whisk together cider vinegar, oil, garlic, basil and tarragon. Season with salt and pepper to taste. Set aside.

2. *Salad:* Place steamer over a pot of boiling water (see Tips, left). Cover and steam green beans for 2 to 3 minutes or until bright green and crisp.

3. In a large serving bowl, combine green beans, red and white kidney beans, chickpeas, red pepper and onion. Add dressing and toss to coat evenly. Cover and refrigerate for at least 2 hours or until chilled, or for up to 4 days.

Variation

Add 1 tbsp (15 mL) finely chopped fresh parsley or 1 tsp (5 mL) dried parsley flakes to the dressing.

Orzo Salad with Lemon and Sage

Tips

Orzo, which resembles large grains of rice, can often be found in a tricolor mix, tinted with natural vegetable dyes. Use this version for a more festive presentation. If you can't find orzo, use any small pasta, such as ditalini or baby shells.

In many locations, green onions are known as scallions.

When ingredients are added to hot pasta, the flavors are absorbed more readily and deeply.

2 cups	orzo or other small pasta (see Tips, left)	500 mL
3 tbsp	freshly squeezed lemon juice	45 mL
1/3 cup	olive oil	75 mL
1/2 cup	thinly sliced green onions (about 4), see Tips, left	125 mL
10	leaves fresh sage, finely chopped (or 2 tsp/10 mL crumbled dried)	10
1	yellow bell pepper, diced (1/2-inch/1 cm dice)	1
2 tbsp	capers, with brine	25 mL
1 tsp	finely grated lemon zest	5 mL
3 tbsp	coarsely chopped fresh Italian parsley	45 mL
1/2 tsp	salt	2 mL
1/4 tsp	freshly ground black pepper	1 mL

1. In a large pot of boiling salted water, cook orzo for 7 to 10 minutes or until tender. Drain and shake in strainer to remove excess water. Transfer to a serving bowl and sprinkle with lemon juice. Toss to coat evenly.

2. Meanwhile, in a skillet, heat olive oil over medium heat for 30 seconds. Add green onions, sage and yellow pepper and cook, stirring, for 1 minute. Stir in capers with brine and lemon zest and cook for 1 minute. Add to orzo mixture. Add parsley, salt and pepper and toss to combine. Let cool to room temperature and serve, or cover and refrigerate for up to 3 days.

Variations

Add 1 cup (250 mL) rinsed drained canned kidney beans when combining the orzo and pepper mixture.

To enhance the Mediterranean flavors in this salad, add 1 cup (250 mL) halved cherry tomatoes and 1/2 cup (125 mL) oil-cured black olives or other olives. Replace the sage with 2 tbsp (25 mL) chopped fresh basil leaves.

This version of the classic salad is filled with high-intensity flavors and, in our opinion, tastes even better than the original.

Tips

When measuring bread cubes, do not pack them tightly in the measuring cup because it will change their shape.

This recipe makes more croutons than needed for this salad. Store the extra at room temperature in an airtight container. They will keep for a week.

Caesar Salad with Capers

❧ *Preheat oven to 375°F (190°C)*
❧ *Large rimmed baking sheet, ungreased*

Half	loaf French bread, day-old or fresh, cut into 1-inch (2.5 cm) cubes (about 3 cups/750 mL), see Tips, left	Half
4 tsp	red wine vinegar	20 mL
1	clove garlic, minced (about 1 tsp/5 mL)	1
1 tbsp	capers, with brine	15 mL
1 tsp	finely grated lemon zest	5 mL
1/8 tsp	freshly ground black pepper	0.5 mL
1/2 cup	soy mayonnaise	125 mL
1 tbsp	coarsely chopped fresh Italian parsley	15 mL
1 tbsp	freshly squeezed lemon juice	15 mL
2 tsp	Dijon mustard	10 mL
12	leaves romaine lettuce, torn into bite-size pieces (about 8 cups/2 L)	12
	Fine sea salt, optional	

1. On baking sheet, spread bread cubes in a single layer. Toast in preheated oven, turning once, for 10 to 12 minutes or until evenly browned. Let cool to room temperature.

2. In a small pot, combine vinegar, garlic, capers, lemon zest and pepper. Cook over medium–low heat for 1 minute or until fragrant but not browned. Remove from heat and set aside.

3. In a bowl, whisk together soy mayonnaise, parsley, lemon juice and mustard. Whisk in vinegar mixture until well blended.

4. In a large salad bowl, combine lettuce and 2 cups (500 mL) of the croutons. Drizzle dressing over salad and toss to coat evenly. Sprinkle with sea salt to taste, if using. Serve immediately.

Quinoa Salad with Grapefruit and Avocado

This salad was inspired by our friend Chef Bruce Tillinghast. The combination of flavors, colors and textures make it a festive dish that can be served year-round. Quinoa, pronounced "KEEN-wah", is actually a seed that is a rich source of protein. Its natural habitat is the high altitudes of the Andes, and it has been called the "lost grain of the Incas." Quinoa has roughly twice the protein of barley, corn and rice and is rich in calcium, iron and vitamin E. It is now making a comeback due to its healthful qualities.

Tips

Quinoa is covered with a resinous coating called saponin, which can actually be used as soap, so it's very important to wash it well. To wash quinoa, submerge it in a bowl of water and swish it around. Transfer to a fine-mesh sieve and rinse thoroughly under cold running water.

To prevent the avocado from discoloring, don't peel or cut it until you are ready to serve the salad.

2 cups	water	500 mL
1 tsp	salt	5 mL
1 cup	quinoa, washed, rinsed and drained (see Tips, left)	250 mL
2 tbsp	chopped fresh mint leaves	25 mL
2 tbsp	freshly squeezed lime juice	25 mL
2 tsp	granulated natural cane sugar or other dry sweetener	10 mL
1/2 tsp	salt	2 mL
Pinch	freshly ground black pepper	Pinch
1/3 cup	vegetable oil	75 mL
1	red grapefruit, peeled, sectioned and each section cut into thirds	1
1	avocado, peeled, pitted and cut in 3/4-inch (2 cm) cubes (see Tips, left)	1
1/3 cup	Pickled Pink Onion Relish (see recipe, page 78)	75 mL

1. In a pot, bring water and salt to a boil over high heat. Add quinoa, stirring to prevent lumps from forming, and return to a boil. Cover, reduce heat to low and simmer for 15 minutes or until tender and liquid is absorbed. Remove from heat and let stand, uncovered, for 5 minutes or until it reaches room temperature. Transfer to a serving bowl.

2. Meanwhile, in a small bowl, whisk together mint, lime juice, sugar, salt and pepper. Whisk in oil. Add grapefruit pieces, avocado and onion relish and toss lightly to coat. Spoon over quinoa, letting dressing drizzle down through the salad. Serve immediately.

Variations

Garnish this salad with a sprinkling of salted roasted pumpkin seeds. Substitute fresh cilantro leaves for the mint.

Substitute 2 oranges or 2 blood oranges for the grapefruit.

Health Salad

*This salad makes a colorful
and flavorful accompaniment
to many meals. It also keeps
very well; in fact, it improves
after a day or two in the
refrigerator.*

Tips

This salad uses a very small
amount of oil compared
to most dressings. If you
prefer, add more oil.

In many locations, green
onions are known as
scallions.

1	large apple (unpeeled), coarsely grated	1
1	small bulb fennel, cored and thinly sliced	1
2 tbsp	freshly squeezed lemon juice	25 mL
6 cups	thinly sliced red or green cabbage (about half a head)	1.5 L
2	carrots, peeled and grated	2
1	red bell pepper, cut into quarters and thinly sliced crosswise	1

DRESSING

3	green onions (white and green parts), finely chopped (see Tips, left)	3
½ cup	cider vinegar	125 mL
3 tbsp	coarsely chopped fresh Italian parsley	45 mL
2 tbsp	olive oil	25 mL
1 tbsp	granulated natural cane sugar or other dry sweetener	15 mL
	Salt and freshly ground black pepper	

1. In a large bowl, combine apple, fennel and lemon juice. Toss to coat. Add cabbage, carrots and red pepper and toss to combine.

2. *Dressing:* In a small bowl, whisk together green onions, vinegar, parsley, olive oil and sugar. Add to cabbage mixture, season with salt and pepper to taste and toss to coat. Cover and refrigerate for at least 2 hours or until flavors are developed, or for up to 2 days.

Variations

If you prefer, substitute 1 tsp (5 mL) of a flavored oil, such as sesame or garlic-infused oil, for the olive oil. For a spicier version, add ½ tsp (2 mL) hot pepper sauce or a pinch of hot pepper flakes to the dressing.

Add 1 tbsp (15 mL) chopped fresh herbs, such as basil leaves, dillweed, oregano leaves or thyme leaves to the cabbage mixture along with the dressing.

If you have leftovers, pack them into a pita with slices of baked tofu (use a prepared version or see recipes, pages 101 and 102) and enjoy a tasty high-fiber, nutrient-rich lunch.

*We think our version of
this salad, which uses a
tofu-based dressing rather
than mayonnaise, improves
upon the original.*

Tips

Cortland, Fuji, Braeburn,
Gala and Red Delicious
apples all work well in
this salad. We like to use
unpeeled apples, not only
because the skin adds
color but also because it is
a great source of fiber.

Squeezing lemon juice
over sliced apples prevents
them from browning when
exposed to air.

Soy creamer is used in the
same way that traditional
cream is. It is rich and
creamy but lower in
saturated fat than its dairy
counterpart.

Waldorf Salad with Cranberries

Food processor or blender

3	crisp red apples (unpeeled), cored, quartered and thinly sliced crosswise (see Tips, left)	3
2 tbsp	freshly squeezed lemon juice (see Tips, left)	25 mL
1/3 cup	dried cranberries or raisins	75 mL
1/4 cup	walnut pieces	50 mL
3	stalks celery, thinly sliced on the diagonal	3

DRESSING

1/3 cup	silken tofu	75 mL
3 tbsp	vegetable oil	45 mL
2 tbsp	soy creamer (see Tips, left)	25 mL
1 tbsp	pure maple syrup	15 mL
1/2 tsp	grated lemon zest	2 mL
1/4 tsp	salt, or to taste	1 mL
1/8 tsp	freshly ground black pepper, or to taste	0.5 mL
2 tbsp	freshly squeezed lemon juice	25 mL

1. In a bowl, combine apples with lemon juice. Add dried cranberries, walnuts and celery.

2. *Dressing:* In a food processor or blender, purée tofu, oil, soy creamer, maple syrup, lemon zest, salt and pepper until smooth. Add lemon juice and blend for 30 seconds or until well combined and smooth. Drizzle dressing over the apple mixture and toss to coat evenly.

Variations

Serve this salad on a bed of mixed greens.

Use half raisins and half dried cranberries.

Substitute chopped pecans for the walnut pieces. Add chopped fresh herbs, such as tarragon, chives or parsley.

Salad of Baby Spinach with Strawberries and Pecans

We love the sweet and tangy flavors in this robust salad. It is also surprisingly good for you; the spinach, strawberries and pecans provide a wide array of nutrients. Use this colorful mix to dress up a meal when entertaining. This recipe makes twice as much dressing as you need, so when you make this salad, you're well on the way to having a second night's dinner prepared.

Tips

We prefer to use a blender rather than a whisk to make this dressing because it ensures that the tofu is completely integrated into the mixture with no lumps. The extra dressing can be refrigerated in an airtight container for up to 1 week. Shake vigorously before using.

Use a shallow wooden serving bowl to maximize the attractiveness of this salad.

To keep the pecans crunchy and the spinach from wilting, don't dress this salad until you are ready to serve it.

➤ Food processor or blender

12 oz	baby spinach	375 g
3 cups	fresh strawberries, hulled and quartered	750 mL
Half	red onion, thinly sliced	Half
1 cup	Spicy Pecans (see recipe, page 38)	250 mL
DRESSING		
1/3 cup	orange juice	75 mL
1/4 cup	strawberry preserves or jam	50 mL
3 tbsp	balsamic vinegar	45 mL
2 tbsp	vegetable oil	25 mL
1 tbsp	silken tofu	15 mL
1	clove garlic, minced	1
3/4 tsp	salt	4 mL

1. In a serving bowl, combine spinach, strawberries, onion and pecans. Toss to combine.

2. In a food processor or blender, combine orange juice, strawberry preserves, vinegar, oil, tofu, garlic and salt. Blend for 45 seconds or until smooth (see Tips, left). Set aside.

3. Just before serving, pour about half of the dressing over the salad and toss to coat evenly, adding more dressing as desired. Save remainder for another use (see Tips, left, and Variation, below).

Variation

Use the leftover dressing to make another delicious salad. In a salad bowl, combine 1 head of red leaf lettuce, washed, dried and torn into bite-size pieces, 1/4 cup (50 mL) slivered almonds; 1 pear (unpeeled), cored and thinly sliced; and 1/4 cup (50 mL) of the leftover dressing. Toss to coat.

This is a great salad for a spring or summer night when you want a light but filling meal that will appeal to the whole family. Or try a two-in-one meal: Taco Salad for those who feel like salad and Make-Your-Own Tacos (see recipe, page 116) for those who prefer tacos.

Tip

Use your favorite prepared salsa or make Tomato and Garlic Salsa (see recipe, page 29).

Taco Salad

1	head iceberg lettuce, torn into bite-size pieces (about 12 cups/3 L)	1
2 cups	crushed seasoned tortilla chips	500 mL
1 cup	canned or home-cooked black beans or red kidney beans (see Legumes, page 13), drained and rinsed	250 mL
1 cup	shredded vegan Cheddar cheese alternative	250 mL
1	red onion, finely chopped (about 1½ cups/375 mL)	1
¾ cup	drained canned pitted black olives, thinly sliced	175 mL
2	tomatoes, halved and thinly sliced	2
¾ cup	tomato salsa (see Tip, left)	175 mL
½ cup	vegan sour cream alternative	125 mL

1. In a large bowl, combine lettuce, tortilla chips, beans, vegan Cheddar cheese, onion, olives, tomatoes and salsa. Toss well. Serve with vegan sour cream on the side.

Variation

For a spicier version of this salad, add ⅓ cup (75 mL) sliced pickled jalapeño peppers, or to taste.

Tips

Use prepared hummus or Hummus with Roasted Red Peppers (see recipe, page 22) in this recipe.

Tortillas come in a variety of flavors, such as spinach, basil or sun-dried tomato, all of which would work well in this recipe.

When packing these wraps in a lunch box, place in a resealable plastic bag to prevent leakage.

Hummus, Avocado and Tomato Wrap

¾ cup	hummus (see Tips, left)	175 mL
4	large tortillas (see Tips, left)	4
4	large leaves lettuce	4
1	large tomato, thinly sliced	1
1	avocado, peeled, pitted and thinly sliced	1

1. Spread 3 tbsp (45 mL) hummus over each tortilla, leaving ¼-inch (0.5 cm) border around the edge. Cover hummus with one lettuce leaf. Place one-quarter of the tomato slices in a line along the bottom of each tortilla, about ½ inch (1 cm) in from the edge. Place one-quarter of the avocado slices on top of each row of tomato slices.

2. One at a time, fold both sides of each tortilla over the filling, then fold the bottom edge over the tomato slices and tightly roll away from you, jelly roll–style. Wrap tightly in foil, if desired, peeling it away as you eat.

Variation

Make this into a pita pocket sandwich. Spread the inside of a halved pita with 3 tbsp (45 mL) hummus, then fill with sliced tomato and avocado, and lettuce leaves, torn in half.

Tips

Tortillas come in a variety of flavors, including spinach, sun-dried tomato and whole wheat. All work well in this recipe.

When packing these wraps in a lunch box, place in a resealable plastic bag to prevent leakage.

Eggplant, Olive and Basil Wrap

❧ *Food processor or blender*

1 cup	Eggplant and Olive Dip (see recipe, page 27)	250 mL
4	large tortillas	4
32	whole basil leaves	32

1. In food processor or blender, purée dip until smooth. Spread ¼ cup (50 mL) of puréed dip over each tortilla, leaving ¼-inch (0.5 cm) border uncovered around the edge.

2. Arrange four basil leaves in a line on top of puréed dip, overlapping as necessary, near bottom edge of each tortilla. Arrange four 4 basil leaves in a line across the middle of the tortilla, parallel to the first line.

3. One at a time, fold both sides of each tortilla over the filling, then fold the bottom edge over the first row of basil leaves and tightly roll away from you, jelly roll–style. Wrap tightly in foil, if desired, peeling it away as you eat.

Variation

Add your favorite sprouts to this wrap, arranging them over the first row of basil leaves. You can also add shredded carrots, next to the first row of basil leaves.

MAKES 4 SERVINGS

This colorful sandwich has a wonderful deep flavor. It makes a great lunch or snack.

Tip

Use prepared baked tofu or Italian–Style Baked Tofu (see recipe, page 102) in this recipe.

Mediterranean Pita Pockets with Tofu and Pickled Onions

4	small whole wheat pitas (each 1 oz/30 g) or 2 large whole wheat pitas (each 2 oz/60 g)	4
½ cup	Olive Spread (see recipe, page 39)	125 mL
1	red bell pepper, thinly sliced	1
20	leaves arugula	20
4 oz	baked tofu (12 thin slices), see Tip, left	125 g
¼ cup	Pickled Pink Onion Relish (see recipe, page 78)	50 mL

1. If using small pitas, insert a knife into edge of each and cut opening around one-third of edge to make pocket. If using larger pitas, cut each in half and gently separate the sides of the pocket, keeping edge attached.

2. For each wrap, spread 2 tbsp (25 mL) Olive Spread over inside bottom of pocket. Place one-quarter of the red pepper slices on top of the olive spread. Place five arugula leaves on top of the peppers. Place three tofu slices over the arugula in an even layer. Finish by scattering one-quarter of the pickled onion relish inside the pocket.

Variations

To make open-faced hors d'oeuvres, dice pepper, shred arugula and coarsely grate tofu. Substitute Herbed Flatbread Chips (see recipe, page 37), small toasts or crackers for the pitas. Spread each piece with Olive Spread, then top with pepper, arugula, tofu, then a small strip of Pickled Pink Onion Relish.

Add 2 tsp (10 mL) of your favorite salad dressing or vinaigrette to each pocket. Remember that the additional liquid might make the pocket soggy if it sits in a lunch bag for too long.

Tofu Pinwheels with Colorful Vegetables

This tasty sandwich is brimming with nutritious vegetables.

Tips

Cut pinwheels on the diagonal for a very colorful presentation.

Tortillas come in a variety of flavors, including spinach, sun-dried tomato and whole wheat. All work well in this recipe.

1	large rectangle of soft lavash (about 11 by 10 inches/28 by 25 cm)	1
⅔ cup	Zesty Tofu Spread (see recipe, page 40)	150 mL
8	leaves red leaf lettuce	8
¾ cup	grated peeled carrot (2 small)	175 mL
2	plum tomatoes or 1 large tomato, seeded, cut into ¼-inch (0.5 cm) thick slices and drained	2
⅔ cup	sprouts (such as alfalfa, radish or bean)	150 mL
⅓ cup	Pickled Pink Onion Relish (see recipe, page 78)	75 mL
1 tbsp	prepared Italian salad dressing	15 mL
	Freshly ground black pepper	

1. Place lavash on work surface with one long edge facing you. Spread with Zesty Tofu Spread, leaving a ½-inch (1 cm) border along the edge farthest from you. Arrange four lettuce leaves, overlapping as necessary, along each long edge of the bread. Sprinkle grated carrot in a line on top of lettuce, about 2 inches (5 cm) in from the bottom edge. Next to the carrot, arrange tomato slices, overlapping, in a line. Sprinkle sprouts in a line next to the tomato slices. Sprinkle onion relish over carrots.

2. Drizzle Italian dressing over carrots and onion relish. Sprinkle pepper to taste over the entire sandwich.

3. Starting with the edge closest to you, roll flatbread away from you into a tight cylinder, jelly roll–style. Slice the roll into four equal pinwheels.

Variation

For an attractive and delicious hors d'oeuvre, use a serrated knife to neatly cut each pinwheel into six bite-size pieces. Insert toothpicks through the center of each piece. Makes 24 hors d'oeuvres.

Soy Bacon, Basil and Tomato Pockets

12	slices soy bacon	12
2	large whole wheat pitas, cut in half	2
3 tbsp	soy mayonnaise	45 mL
¼ cup	fresh basil leaves	50 mL
1	large tomato, thinly sliced	1
	Freshly ground black pepper, optional	

1. Cook bacon strips according to package directions. Let cool slightly.

2. Carefully separate pitas to open pockets. Spread one-quarter of the soy mayonnaise over inside bottom of each pita half. For each pocket, top mayonnaise with one-quarter each of the basil leaves and tomato slices. Place 3 strips of bacon over tomatoes. Season with pepper to taste, if using. Repeat with remaining ingredients.

Variations

Chop the basil leaves and stir into the mayonnaise, then spread over the pitas.

Soy Bacon, Basil and Tomato Sandwich: If you prefer a more traditional presentation, substitute 8 slices whole wheat bread, toasted, for the pitas. Continue with Step 2.

Pickled Pink Onion Relish

Tip

The color of this relish will deepen with time. Any juice leftover once the onions have been used up can be used to make tasty salad dressings and marinades.

6 cups	water	1.5 L
1 tsp	salt	5 mL
1	red onion, cut in half from stem to root, then crosswise and thinly sliced	1
½ cup	seasoned rice vinegar	125 mL

1. In a pot over high heat, bring water and salt to a boil. Add onion and return to a boil (about 45 seconds). Drain and immediately transfer to a nonreactive container. Add vinegar and toss to coat evenly.

2. Let cool to room temperature. Cover and refrigerate for 2 hours or until chilled and deep pink.

Variations

Add ½ tsp (2 mL) of your favorite dried herb, such as thyme leaves, tarragon or basil leaves, along with the vinegar.

In place of seasoned rice vinegar, use cider vinegar and 2 tsp (10 mL) granulated natural cane sugar or other dry sweetener.

Use ½ cup (125 mL) freshly squeezed lemon juice or another flavored vinegar instead of the rice vinegar to steep the onions. Add 2 tsp (10 mL) granulated natural cane sugar or other dry sweetener. We do not recommend balsamic vinegar, as the dark brown color overpowers the pink onions.

Casseroles, Tofu and Legumes

Spaghetti and Soyballs

Tips

Substitute 14 oz (420 g) soy ground meat alternative for the meatless meatballs. Pinch off small pieces and roll into balls approximately 1 inch (2.5 cm) in diameter.

Soy meat alternatives come in a variety of textures. Those found in the refrigerated section of your supermarket tend to be moister than those found in the frozen section. The moist versions are easiest to work with when forming soyballs.

Use prepared tomato sauce or make your own (see recipe, page 154).

8 oz	spaghetti	250 g
1/4 cup	dry bread crumbs	50 mL
2 tbsp	coarsely chopped fresh oregano leaves (or 2 tsp/10 mL dried)	25 mL
1 tbsp	coarsely chopped fresh parsley (or 1 tsp/5 mL dried)	15 mL
1 tbsp	whole wheat or unbleached all-purpose flour	15 mL
1	package (14 oz/420 g) meatless meatballs (see Tips, left)	1
4 cups	tomato sauce (see Tips, left)	1 L
3 tbsp	olive oil	45 mL
	Grated vegan Parmesan cheese alternative, optional	

1. In a pot of boiling salted water, cook spaghetti for 8 minutes or until tender to the bite. Drain.

2. Meanwhile, in a bowl, combine bread crumbs, oregano, parsley and flour. Add meatballs and toss until evenly coated. Transfer to a plate, shaking off excess crumb mixture. Set aside.

3. In a pot, heat tomato sauce over low heat until heated through.

4. Meanwhile, in a large nonstick skillet, heat oil over medium–high heat for 30 seconds. Add meatballs and cook, turning, until lightly browned and crispy. Using a slotted spoon, transfer to tomato sauce. Simmer, uncovered, for 5 minutes or until heated through.

5. Divide hot spaghetti among plates. Spoon soyballs and sauce over top.

Pasta Bake

This simple but hearty meal
is sure to be a hit with the
whole family. It reheats well,
so don't worry about having
leftovers.

Tips

Vegan Cheddar cheese
alternative is excellent
for shredding, but not
all brands melt well. You
may need to try a few
before finding one that
works to your satisfaction
in this recipe.

When minced, 3 cloves of
garlic makes about 1 tbsp
(15 mL).

Substitute 1 tsp (5 mL)
dried basil, oregano or
parsley for the fresh herbs,
if desired.

- Preheat oven to 350°F (180°C)
- 8-cup (2 L) casserole dish, greased
- Food processor or blender

8 oz	rotini or other short ridged pasta, such as penne or rigatoni	250 g
SAUCE		
1	can (28 oz/796 mL) diced tomatoes, with juices	1
1 tbsp	olive oil	15 mL
3	cloves garlic, minced	3
1 cup	sliced pitted black olives	250 mL
3	Italian-style soy sausages, cut into 1/4-inch (0.5 cm) slices	3
2 tbsp	tomato paste	25 mL
1 tbsp	chopped fresh basil leaves (see Tips, left)	15 mL
1 tbsp	chopped fresh oregano leaves	15 mL
1 tbsp	chopped fresh parsley	15 mL
1/2 tsp	freshly ground black pepper	2 mL
1/4 tsp	hot pepper flakes, or to taste	1 mL
1 1/2 cups	shredded vegan Cheddar cheese alternative	375 mL

1. In a large pot of boiling salted water, cook pasta for 8 minutes or until tender to the bite. Drain.

2. *Sauce:* In a food processor or blender, purée tomatoes with juices until smooth. Set aside.

3. In a large skillet, heat oil over medium heat for 30 seconds. Add garlic and cook, stirring, for 2 minutes or until fragrant but not browned. Stir in puréed tomatoes, olives, soy sausages, tomato paste, basil, oregano, parsley, black pepper and hot pepper flakes. Reduce heat to medium-low, cover, and cook for 10 minutes or until thickened.

4. Add pasta and half of the cheese alternative and stir until evenly coated. Pour into prepared dish. Sprinkle remaining cheese alternative evenly over top. Cover with foil and bake in preheated oven for 15 minutes. Remove foil and bake for 10 minutes longer or until hot and bubbly.

Variation

Add any of your favorite vegetables, such as broccoli or sliced mushrooms, along with the tomatoes.

Three-Bean Chili

Tips

Because can sizes vary, we provide a range of amounts for beans in our recipes. If you're using 19-oz (540 mL) cans, add a bit of chili powder to taste.

Use diced tomatoes with or without seasonings.

This dish can be frozen for up to 2 months in an airtight container.

1 tbsp	vegetable oil	15 mL
1	large onion, coarsely chopped	1
1	red bell pepper, cut into 1-inch (2.5 cm) cubes	1
2	cloves garlic, minced (about 2 tsp/10 mL)	2
1 1/2 tbsp	chili powder	22 mL
1 1/2 tsp	ground cumin	7 mL
1/2 tsp	dried oregano leaves	2 mL
1/2 tsp	ground cinnamon	2 mL
1/2 tsp	ground allspice	2 mL
1/4 tsp	hot pepper flakes	1 mL
2 cups	vegetable stock	500 mL
1/2 cup	tomato paste	125 mL
1	can (14 to 19 oz/398 to 540 mL) black beans, drained and rinsed (see Tips, left), or 1 cup (250 mL) dried black beans, soaked, cooked and drained (see Legumes, page 13)	1
1	can (14 to 19 oz/398 to 540 mL) red kidney beans, drained and rinsed, or 1 cup (250 mL) dried red kidney beans, soaked, cooked and drained	1
1	can (14 to 19 oz/398 to 540 mL) navy or white kidney beans, drained and rinsed, or 1 cup (250 mL) dried navy or white kidney beans, soaked, cooked and drained	1
1	can (28 oz/796 mL) diced tomatoes, with juices (see Tips, left)	1
1 tbsp	red wine vinegar	15 mL

1. In a large pot, heat oil over medium heat for 30 seconds. Add onion and red pepper and cook, stirring, for 3 minutes or until softened. Add garlic and cook, stirring, for 1 minute. Add chili powder, cumin, oregano, cinnamon, allspice and hot pepper flakes and cook, stirring, for 1 minute.

2. Add vegetable stock and increase heat to medium–high. Bring to a simmer and cook for 5 minutes or until pepper is very soft. Add tomato paste and stir well. Add black, red kidney and navy beans, tomatoes and vinegar. Return to a boil. Reduce heat to low, cover and simmer for 35 minutes or until thickened.

Variation

For a more substantial version of this chili, add 6 oz (175 g) soy ground meat alternative. In a skillet, heat 1 tbsp (15 mL) of olive oil over medium–high heat. Add meat alternative and reduce heat to medium. Cook, stirring frequently, for 5 minutes or until heated through. Add to chili along with the vinegar.

Shepherd's Pie

Tip

Frozen mixed vegetables
come in several varieties.
Those that include corn,
green beans and peas work
best in this dish.

❧ Preheat oven to 375°F (190°C)
❧ 8-cup (2 L) casserole dish, greased

1 tbsp	olive oil	15 mL
1	onion, finely chopped	1
1 cup	vegetable stock	250 mL
12 oz	soy ground meat alternative	375 g
10 oz	frozen mixed vegetables (about 1½ cups/375 mL), thawed and drained (see Tip, left)	300 g
2 cups	Garlic Mashed Potatoes (see recipe, page 147)	500 mL
1½ cups	shredded vegan Cheddar cheese alternative	375 mL
	Salt and freshly ground black pepper	

1. In a large skillet, heat oil over medium heat for 30 seconds. Add onion and cook, stirring, for 3 minutes or until softened. Add vegetable stock and cook for 3 minutes. Add soy ground meat alternative. Reduce heat to low, cover and cook for 10 minutes or until heated through.

2. Add vegetables and stir well. Cook for 5 minutes or until heated through. Transfer to prepared casserole dish. Top with mashed potatoes, spreading evenly. Sprinkle vegan Cheddar cheese alternative over top.

3. Bake in preheated oven for 25 minutes or until potatoes and cheese form a soft crust on top.

Stuffed Pepper Boats

You'll get a complete meal in one pepper boat (or more, for those with healthy appetites). Accompany these boats with a salad and you have all the elements of a healthy and satisfying meal. While this is one of our more complex recipes to prepare, it's worth the work. If you end up with leftovers, the next day's meal preparation will be a breeze.

Tip

If you're using canned diced tomatoes without seasoning, add 1 tsp (5 mL) dried oregano leaves, ½ tsp (2 mL) dried basil leaves and ¼ tsp (1 mL) freshly ground black pepper to the vegetable mixture to enhance the flavor.

➤ Preheat oven to 375°F (190°C)
➤ 13-by 9-inch (3 L) baking dish, greased

1 cup	brown rice	250 mL
5	large green or red bell peppers or a mixture of both	5
2½ tbsp	olive oil, divided	32 mL
2 tbsp	balsamic vinegar	25 mL
1	large onion, finely chopped	1
2	cloves garlic, minced (about 2 tsp/10 mL)	2
8 oz	mushrooms, finely chopped	250 g
1	can (28 oz/796 mL) seasoned diced tomatoes, with juices	1
3	soy sausages, cut into ¼-inch (0.5 cm) slices	3
	Salt	
¾ cup	shredded vegan Cheddar cheese alternative	175 mL

1. Cook brown rice according to package instructions.

2. Meanwhile, cut peppers in half lengthwise. Cut out stem, core and seeds and discard. In a small bowl, whisk together 1½ tsp (7 mL) oil and balsamic vinegar. Place pepper halves in prepared baking dish and brush lightly on both sides with vinegar mixture. Bake for 20 minutes or until just starting to soften.

3. In a large skillet, heat 2 tbsp (25 mL) oil over medium heat for 30 seconds. Add onion and cook, stirring, for 3 minutes or until softened. Add garlic and cook, stirring, for 1 minute. Add mushrooms. Reduce heat to low, cover and simmer for 3 to 4 minutes or until mushrooms are soft. Stir in tomatoes, soy sausages and salt to taste. Simmer, uncovered, for 10 minutes or until flavors are blended. Stir in rice.

4. Remove peppers from oven and let cool for 5 minutes. Pack each pepper boat with rice mixture to form a mound. Sprinkle shredded vegan Cheddar cheese alternative over top of stuffing. Bake for 20 minutes longer or until peppers are soft and wrinkled.

This is a perfect dish to serve to company. Not only do its vibrant colors jump off the plate, but it is also packed with vitamins and protein. As delicious as this dish is freshly made, it tastes even better the next day.

Tips

Some udon noodles come precooked. They may need only to be soaked briefly in hot water, then drained.

Hot sesame oil can be found in Asian markets and the Asian foods section of major supermarkets. As an alternative, increase the amount of sesame oil to 1¼ tsp (6 mL) and add ¼ tsp (1 mL) hot pepper flakes along with the green onions.

Look for frozen Asian mushroom medley and spicy tofu chunks in major grocery stores, natural foods stores or Asian markets. If these ingredients are not available, you can use 4 oz (125 g) button mushrooms, sliced, and one 14-oz (420 g) can of straw mushrooms instead of the medley. For the tofu, substitute Asian-Style Baked Tofu (see recipe, page 101) and add a dash of chili or hot sesame oil.

Udon Noodles with Spicy Tofu and Asian Vegetables

10 oz	udon noodles (see Tips, left)	300 g
1 tbsp	vegetable oil	15 mL
12 oz	frozen Asian mushroom medley (see Tips, left)	375 g
1	red bell pepper, cut into long strips ½ inch (1 cm) thick	1
1 cup	snow peas, ends trimmed and cut in half	250 mL
8 oz	spicy tofu chunks, cubed (1 inch/2.5 cm), see Tips, left	250 g
¾ cup	chopped green onions (green and white parts)	175 mL

SAUCE

½ cup	soy sauce	125 mL
¼ cup	distilled white vinegar	50 mL
1 tsp	granulated natural cane sugar	5 mL
1 tsp	sesame oil	5 mL
¼ tsp	hot sesame oil (see Tips, left)	1 mL

1. Cook udon noodles according to package directions, if necessary. Drain and set aside.

2. *Sauce:* In a bowl, whisk together soy sauce, vinegar, sugar, sesame oil and hot sesame oil. Set aside.

3. In a large nonstick skillet or wok, heat vegetable oil over medium heat for 30 seconds. Add mushrooms and pepper and cook, stirring frequently, for 5 minutes. Add snow peas and cook for 3 minutes or until tender-crisp. Stir in tofu and green onions. Reduce heat to low and cook, stirring, for 2 minutes or until hot.

4. Add udon noodles and half of the sauce to the skillet. Mix well and cook, stirring, for 2 minutes or until noodles are hot and vegetables are coated with sauce. Transfer to a serving dish. Serve remaining sauce on the side.

These tasty nuggets do double duty as finger food for a party or a great main course.

Tip

You can find smoked barbecued tofu in most major supermarkets or natural foods stores. If you can't find it, use the same amount of extra-firm tofu, cubed. Place the cubes on a double layer of paper towels. Let drain for 20 minutes. Pour off water and set tofu aside.

Barbecued Tofu Nuggets

❧ *Preheat oven to 375°F (190°C)*
❧ *Rimmed baking sheet, greased*

6 oz	smoked barbecued tofu, cut into 12 cubes (see Tip, left)	175 g
1/3 cup	barbecue sauce	75 mL
1 1/2 cups	finely crushed plain potato chips or barbecue-flavor potato chips	375 mL

1. Pat tofu dry with paper towels and brush all over with barbecue sauce. Place potato chips in a bowl. One at a time, drop cubes into potato chips, lightly tossing to ensure all sides are coated.

2. Place nuggets on prepared pan, 2 to 3 inches (5 to 7.5 cm) apart. Bake in preheated oven for 12 minutes or until hot and crispy. Let cool on pan for 1 minute. Using a metal spatula, transfer to a serving platter.

Variations

Substitute your favorite flavored potato chips, tortilla chips or wheat crackers for the plain or barbecue-flavored chips.

Substitute 1/3 cup (75 mL) soy mayonnaise for the barbecue sauce.

Polenta with Eggplant and Sun-Dried Tomatoes

Although this recipe has a number of steps, it is actually very easy to make. For convenience, prepare some of the ingredients in advance.

Tips

Polenta and medium-grain cornmeal are one and the same. Look for either in your market.

For a more intense garlic flavor, use an equal amount of garlic–infused oil in place of the garlic powder.

Use prepared tomato sauce or make your own (see recipe, page 154).

This recipe can be assembled up to 2 days ahead of time. Cover tightly and refrigerate. Increase baking time by 5 minutes.

Preheat oven to 350°F (180°C)
Two 15-by 10-inch (37.5 by 25 cm) rimmed baking sheets, greased
13-by 9-inch (3 L) baking dish, greased

1	large eggplant, cut into ¼-inch (0.5 cm) slices	1
1 tbsp	kosher or coarse sea salt	15 mL
4 cups	water	1 L
1 cup	medium-grain cornmeal (see Tips)	250 mL
3 tbsp	finely chopped fresh oregano leaves (or 1 tbsp/15 mL dried), divided	45 mL
2 tbsp	finely chopped fresh basil leaves (or 2 tsp/10 mL dried), divided	25 mL
2 tsp	garlic powder, divided	10 mL
2 tbsp	olive oil (see Tips, left)	25 mL
½ cup	finely chopped drained oil-packed sun-dried tomatoes, divided	125 mL
3 cups	tomato sauce (see Tips, left), divided	750 mL
1½ cups	shredded vegan Cheddar cheese alternative	375 mL

1. In a colander over the sink, toss eggplant with salt. Let drain for 20 minutes. Rinse, drain and pat dry.

2. Meanwhile, in a saucepan, bring water to a boil. Remove from heat and gradually whisk in cornmeal, whisking constantly. Whisk in 1½ tbsp (22 mL) oregano, 1 tbsp (15 mL) basil and 1 tsp (5 mL) garlic powder. Return saucepan to medium heat and cook, whisking constantly, for 2 minutes or until the surface starts to bubble. Remove from heat and let cool for 10 to 15 minutes or until firm.

3. In a small bowl, combine remaining oregano, basil and garlic powder.

4. On one prepared baking sheet, arrange eggplant slices in a single layer. Brush both sides with olive oil and sprinkle with oregano mixture. Bake for 25 minutes or until eggplant is soft and fragrant. Remove from oven and set aside. Increase oven temperature to 475°F (240°C).

5. Over remaining prepared baking sheet, spread cooled polenta in an even layer, approximately ¼ inch (0.5 cm) thick. Bake polenta for 10 minutes or until lightly browned around the edges (watch to ensure it doesn't overcook). Reduce oven temperature to 400°F (200°C).

6. Let polenta cool on pan for 5 minutes. Cut in half crosswise and carefully place one half in the bottom of prepared baking dish. Cover with half of the eggplant slices and half of the sun-dried tomatoes. Spread with half of the tomato sauce. Top with remaining polenta, eggplant, sun-dried tomatoes, then sauce. Sprinkle shredded Cheddar cheese alternative over the top. Bake for 25 minutes or until hot and bubbling. Let cool in dish for 5 minutes before serving.

Here's a great way to use up leftover cooked rice. It's easy to make, delicious and nutritious. Served with a salad, this is a great solution for a night when you don't feel like cooking but want a home-cooked meal.

Tip

After increasing the oven temperature, watch carefully. You want the topping to brown but not burn.

Baked Beans and Rice Casserole

❧ *Preheat oven to 375°F (190°C)*
❧ *8-cup (2 L) casserole dish, greased*

2	strips soy bacon	2
2	cans (each 14 to 16 oz/398 to 480 mL) vegetarian baked beans	2
½ tsp	chili powder	2 mL
½ tsp	hot pepper sauce, or to taste	2 mL
¼ tsp	hot pepper flakes, or to taste	1 mL
2 cups	cooked jasmine or white rice	500 mL
½ cup	dry bread crumbs	125 mL
2 tbsp	soy margarine, melted	25 mL

1. In a small nonstick skillet, cook soy bacon according to package directions until crisp. Let cool for 3 minutes. Break into small pieces that resemble bacon bits.

2. In prepared dish, combine bacon pieces, baked beans, chili powder, hot pepper sauce and pepper flakes. Stir in cooked rice. Sprinkle with bread crumbs and drizzle margarine over top.

3. Bake in preheated oven for 25 minutes or until hot and bubbling. Increase oven temperature to 500°F (260°C). Cook for 2 to 3 minutes or until topping is browned. Let stand for 3 to 5 minutes before serving.

Variation

Replace soy bacon with veggie franks. Use 2 franks and cut into ½-inch (1 cm) thick slices, then cut each slice in half.

Curried Chickpeas

This recipe requires very little effort, takes less than half an hour from stove top to table and makes a quick family supper. Served with steamed or sticky rice and a salad, it's a particular favorite of kids.

Tips

Precooking curry powder in oil helps maximize its flavor and mitigate any potential harshness. In this recipe, we have cooked it with other ingredients for convenience.

Although coconut milk adds the best flavor to this dish, you can replace all or a portion of it with almond milk or any other non-dairy beverage if you prefer. You can make your own coconut-flavored milk by combining ½ cup (125 mL) unsweetened coconut flakes and 1¾ cups (425 mL) of your dairy-free beverage of choice. Bring to a simmer, cover and remove from heat. Let steep for 5 minutes, then strain. Reserve coconut to use as a garnish, along with or instead of the cilantro.

2 tbsp	vegetable oil	25 mL
1	Spanish onion, thinly sliced (about 1½ cups/375 mL)	1
3	garlic cloves, minced (about 1 tbsp/15 mL)	3
1 tbsp	curry powder	15 mL
1	can (14 oz/398 mL) coconut milk	1
1	can (14 to 19 oz/398 to 540 mL) chickpeas, drained and rinsed, or 1 cup (250 mL) dried chickpeas, soaked, cooked and drained (see Legumes, page 13)	1
1 lb	frozen mixed bell peppers, thawed, or fresh bell peppers, cut into 2-inch by ¼-inch (5 cm by 0.5 cm) strips	500 g
2 tbsp	tomato paste	25 mL
1 tbsp	packed brown sugar or granulated natural cane sugar	15 mL
1 tbsp	freshly squeezed lemon juice	15 mL
1 tsp	salt, or to taste	5 mL
Pinch	hot pepper flakes or dash hot pepper sauce	Pinch
2 tbsp	chopped fresh cilantro leaves or parsley, optional	25 mL

1. In a large skillet, heat oil over medium heat for about 30 seconds. Add onion and cook, stirring, for 3 minutes or until softened. Add garlic and curry powder and cook, stirring, for 1 minute.

2. Stir in coconut milk, chickpeas, peppers, tomato paste, brown sugar, lemon juice, salt and hot pepper flakes and bring to a boil. Reduce heat and simmer, uncovered, for 20 to 25 minutes or until sauce is thickened and vegetables are tender. Serve sprinkled with cilantro, if using.

Spinach and Tofu Dumplings

This recipe is now in its third generation of sharing. Previously known as Mrs. Sebastiani's Malfatti, it was handed down from a friend's mother, written in beautiful 1950s penmanship. We have updated it for the new millennium. Serve hot or at room temperature.

❧*Preheat oven to 350°F (180°C)*
❧*Food processor*
❧*12-cup (3 L) baking dish, greased*

Tips

If spinach is only available in 10-oz (300 g) packages, use 1½ packages in this recipe and reserve the remainder for another use.

To drain thawed frozen spinach, place it in a fine-mesh strainer and press down with a wooden spoon until all the moisture is removed. If you don't have a fine-mesh strainer, you can use your hands. Working with a small handful of spinach at a time, gently squeeze four or five times to remove excess liquid. Repeat until all the spinach has been drained.

When using egg replacer, prepare according to package directions. Egg replacers vary in their ratios of powder to water.

Use homemade tomato sauce (see recipe, page 154) or a store-bought version.

This dish can be made a day ahead. Complete Step 5. Cover tightly and refrigerate. When ready to cook, remove cover and proceed with Step 6, adding 10 minutes to the baking time.

Quarter	loaf (about 5 inches/12.5 cm long) French bread, torn into a few large chunks	Quarter
½ cup	warm water	125 mL
1 tbsp	olive oil	15 mL
Half	onion, finely chopped	Half
1	small clove garlic, finely chopped	1
1 lb	frozen chopped spinach, thawed and drained (see Tips, left)	500 g
½ cup	Italian-Style Baked Tofu (see recipe, page 102), grated	125 mL
¾ tsp	salt	4 mL
½ tsp	dried basil leaves	2 mL
¼ tsp	freshly ground black pepper	1 mL
	Egg replacer for 2 eggs, prepared according to package directions (see Tips, left)	
½ cup	dry bread crumbs	125 mL
	All-purpose flour	
2½ cups	tomato sauce (see Tips, left)	625 mL

1. In a bowl, soak bread in warm water for 1 minute. Squeeze dry, discarding excess water. Set aside.

2. In a skillet, heat oil over medium heat for 30 seconds. Add onion and cook, stirring, for 3 minutes or until softened. Add garlic and cook, stirring, for 1 minute. Add spinach and cook, stirring, for 2 minutes or until liquid is evaporated. Transfer to a large bowl.

3. Add reserved bread, tofu, salt, basil, pepper and egg replacer and stir to blend.

4. In a food processor, process mixture, in batches, pulsing about 10 times per batch, to make a uniform, coarsely textured dough. (You'll need to scrape down the sides of the bowl to ensure that the mixture is well blended.) Return dough to a bowl and stir in bread crumbs.

5. In a large pot, bring 12 cups (3 L) of water and 1 tbsp (15 mL) of salt to boil. With lightly floured hands, shape small pieces of dough into cylinder-shaped dumplings, about 3- by 1-inch (7.5 by 2.5 cm). Place on a lightly floured surface. Drop dumplings, a few at a time, into boiling water. Reduce heat until the water is barely simmering (this will vary depending on your stove) and cook for 4 to 6 minutes or until dumplings float to the surface. Remove with a slotted spoon and place in prepared baking dish. Return water to a boil between batches. Spoon tomato sauce over dumplings.

6. Bake in preheated oven for 20 minutes or until hot and bubbling.

This dish was created for Beth's stepdaughter, Val, who is originally from Haiti, to satisfy her longing for Haitian cuisine. The leftovers make great snack food rolled up with Chunky Guacamole (see recipe, page 28) or vegetables in a tortilla.

Tips

If you're making this dish for heat lovers, accompany it with hot pepper sauce as a condiment.

We like to serve this dish with Health Salad (see recipe, page 69), which we enhance with extra white vinegar (about 1 tbsp/15 mL per cup/250 mL of salad). The result is reminiscent of a spicy carrot-and-cabbage condiment served in Haiti.

Caribbean Rice and Beans

2 tbsp	olive oil	25 mL
1	onion, finely chopped	1
2	cloves garlic, minced (about 2 tsp/10 mL)	2
1½ cups	long-grain white rice	375 mL
1	bay leaf	1
6	whole cloves (or ¼ tsp/1 mL ground cloves)	6
1½ tbsp	tomato paste	22 mL
½ tsp	ground allspice	2 mL
½ tsp	salt, optional	2 mL
¼ tsp	hot pepper flakes	1 mL
1	can (14 oz/398 mL) coconut milk	1
1¼ cups	water	300 mL
1	can (14 to 19 oz/398 to 540 mL) red kidney beans, drained and rinsed, or 1 cup (250 mL) dried kidney beans, soaked, cooked and rinsed (see Legumes, page 13)	1

1. In a heavy pot, heat oil over medium heat for 30 seconds. Add onion and cook, stirring, for 3 minutes or until softened. Add garlic and cook, stirring, for 30 seconds. Add rice and cook, stirring, for 4 minutes or until coated and hot. Remove from heat.

2. Add bay leaf, cloves, tomato paste, allspice, salt, if using, and hot pepper flakes and stir well. Stir in coconut milk and water. Increase heat to medium–high and bring to a boil, stirring often to prevent sticking. Reduce heat to low, cover and simmer for 18 minutes or until rice is tender and liquid is absorbed.

3. Add kidney beans and stir well. Cover and cook for 2 minutes. Remove from heat. Discard bay leaf and cloves. Serve piping hot.

Sesame Noodles with Tofu

Tips

Use all-natural, nonhomogenized peanut butter for best results.

Make sure to taste the sauce when mixing, as the amount of sugar may need to be adjusted based on the brand of peanut butter you use. Some are saltier than others.

You can find hot sesame oil in Asian markets or well-stocked supermarkets. If you can't find it, use regular sesame oil.

In many locations, green onions are known as scallions.

This recipe uses half a batch of Asian-Style Baked Tofu (see recipe, page 101). If you prefer, substitute prepared baked tofu with Asian seasonings. You can find it in the refrigerator section of many supermarkets.

10 oz	rice noodles	300 g
6 cups	hot water	1.5 L
½ cup	coarsely chopped green onions (white and green parts), divided (see Tips, left)	125 mL
⅓ cup	natural nonhomogenized peanut butter (see Tips, left)	75 mL
¼ cup	sesame oil	50 mL
3 tbsp	low-sodium soy sauce	45 mL
1 ½ tbsp	tahini	22 mL
1 tbsp	granulated natural cane sugar, or to taste	15 mL
Dash	hot sesame oil, or to taste (see Tips, left)	Dash
8 oz	Asian-Style Baked Tofu (see Tips, left), cubed (1-inch/2.5 cm cubes)	250 g
1	cucumber, peeled and sliced into 2½- by ½-inch (6 by 1 cm) strips	1

1. In a bowl, soak noodles in hot water for 20 minutes or until soft (or prepare according to package directions). Drain and transfer to a large serving bowl.

2. In a small bowl, combine all but 2 tbsp (25 mL) of the green onions, peanut butter, sesame oil, soy sauce, tahini, sugar and hot sesame oil. (This should become a thick, light brown sauce. If your mixture is too thick, stir in up to 1 tbsp/15 mL water.) Pour about two-thirds of the sauce over noodles. Add tofu and gently toss to coat evenly.

3. Place the cucumber slices around the perimeter of the noodles. Pour the remaining sauce over top and sprinkle with remaining green onions.

Variation

Garnish with 2 tbsp (25 mL) chopped peanuts and a sprig of parsley.

Mexican Casserole

Tips

If you prefer, make your own salsa rather than using a prepared version (see Tomato and Garlic Salsa, page 29).

You will need 1 cup (250 mL) crushed tortilla chips to sprinkle over the casserole along with the vegan Cheddar cheese alternative. Before beginning this recipe, scoop out a large handful of chips and place them in a plastic or paper bag. Crush by hand or with a rolling pin. Repeat until you have 1 cup (250 mL) crushed chips, then set aside. Use the remaining whole chips to make two inner layers of the casserole. You may have slightly more than you need, so save any leftovers for a snack.

The tortilla chips and salsa you use make a big difference in this recipe. If you like spicy food, then hot salsa with spicy tortilla chips will be perfect. If you're heat-averse, use milder versions. The vegan Cheddar cheese alternative you use will also affect results, as some types melt better than others.

Preheat oven to 350°F (180°C)
8-cup (2 L) casserole dish, greased

2 tbsp	vegetable oil	25 mL
1	large onion, finely chopped	1
12 oz	soy ground meat alternative	375 g
2 cups	salsa (see Tips, left)	500 mL
1	bag (8 oz/250 g) seasoned tortilla chips (see Tips, left)	1
1 cup	refried beans	250 mL
1 cup	shredded vegan Cheddar cheese alternative	250 mL

1. In a large nonstick skillet, heat oil over medium heat for 30 seconds. Add onion and cook, stirring, for 3 minutes or until softened. Add soy meat alternative and reduce heat to low. Cook, stirring, for 4 minutes or until heated through. Stir in salsa, cover and simmer for 5 minutes.

2. Spread a layer of tortilla chips evenly over bottom of prepared dish. Cover with half of the refried beans, then half of the salsa mixture. Repeat layers once. Crush remaining tortilla chips and sprinkle over dish. Sprinkle with vegan Cheddar cheese alternative.

3. Bake in preheated oven, uncovered, for 25 minutes or until mixture is hot and bubbling and the crushed chips are lightly toasted.

Shepherd's Pie *(page 84)*

Overleaf: Quinoa Salad with Grapefruit and Avocado *(page 68)*

Savory Artichoke Pie

Tips

You can make your own pie crust (see recipe, page 174) or use a prepared version. Although many store-bought pie crusts are naturally vegan, some are made with butter, eggs or lard. Check the ingredient list to make sure you're purchasing a vegan version.

If your bouillon cube is very dry, soften it by placing it in a small cup and sprinkling with a teaspoon (5 mL) of boiling water. Set aside for 1 minute, then pour off excess water. It is ready for use.

If the rim of the pie crust begins to get very brown before the baking is finished, cover it with strips of foil.

Curried Vegetables with Tofu
(page 98)

Preheat oven to 375°F (190°C)
Food processor

2 tbsp	olive oil	25 mL
1	large Spanish onion, thinly sliced (about 2 cups/500 mL)	1
3	cloves garlic, minced (about 1 tbsp/15 mL)	3
2 tbsp	chopped fresh basil leaves (or 2 tsp/10 mL dried)	25 mL
4	canned or bottled artichoke hearts, drained, gently squeezed and cut into 6 wedges each	4
1/4 tsp	hot pepper flakes	1 mL
12 oz	firm silken tofu, lightly drained	375 g
1	cube vegan vegetable bouillon (or 1 1/2 tsp/7 mL powdered vegetable bouillon)	1
1/4 tsp	hot pepper sauce	1 mL
	Salt and freshly ground black pepper, or to taste	
1	9-inch (23 cm) pie crust, baked (see Tip, left)	1
2 tsp	chopped fresh Italian parsley, optional	10 mL

1. In a large skillet, heat oil over medium–high heat for 30 seconds. Add onion and cook, stirring, for 8 minutes or until lightly browned and soft. Add garlic and basil and cook, stirring, for 1 minute. Remove from heat and stir in artichokes and hot pepper flakes.

2. In a food processor, purée tofu, bouillon cube and hot pepper sauce. Season with salt and pepper to taste. Use a rubber spatula to scrape down the sides of the bowl and continue to blend until completely smooth.

3. Spread half of the tofu mixture in baked pie crust. Arrange half of the artichoke mixture evenly over tofu. Spread remaining tofu mixture over top, pressing lightly with a spatula to eliminate any air pockets. Arrange remaining artichoke mixture evenly over top.

4. Bake in preheated oven for 30 to 35 minutes or until tofu mixture is firmly set and topping is lightly browned. Let cool on a rack for 5 to 10 minutes. Sprinkle with parsley, if using, and season with salt and pepper to taste. Serve hot or at room temperature.

If you're looking for a healthy, flavorful meal for family and friends, serve this dish over hot fluffy jasmine or basmati rice. Or, for a change, try it with Coconut Rice (see recipe, page 131).

Tips

Fried bean curd can be found in natural food stores or Asian markets. It comes prepackaged in cubes or triangles. Because of its light and airy consistency, it absorbs flavors very nicely.

Because can sizes vary, we provide a range of amounts for beans in our recipes. If you're using 19-oz (540 mL) cans, add a bit of curry powder to taste.

Curried Vegetables with Tofu

2 tsp	vegetable oil	10 mL
1	sweet onion (such as Vidalia), coarsely chopped	1
1	red bell pepper, cut into 1- by ½-inch (2.5 by 1 cm) strips	1
2 tsp	curry powder	10 mL
½ tsp	ground ginger	2 mL
2 cups	broccoli florets	500 mL
2 cups	cauliflower florets	500 mL
1 cup	vegetable stock	250 mL
2 or 3	carrots, cut into ¼-inch (0.5 cm) thick slices (1 cup/250 mL)	2 or 3
1	can (14 to 19 oz/398 to 540 mL) chickpeas, drained and rinsed, or 1 cup (250 mL) dried chickpeas, soaked, cooked and drained (see Legumes, page 13)	1
10 oz	firm tofu, cubed (1 inch/2.5 cm) or fried bean curd (see Tips, left)	300 g
½ cup	vanilla-flavor soy milk	125 mL
3 tbsp	unsweetened shredded coconut	45 mL
2 tsp	granulated natural cane sugar	10 mL
	Salt and freshly ground black pepper	

1. In a large nonstick skillet, heat oil over medium heat for 30 seconds. Add onion and cook, stirring, for 3 minutes or until softened. Add red pepper, curry powder and ginger and cook, stirring, for 1 minute. Add broccoli, cauliflower, vegetable stock and carrots and cook, stirring, for 4 to 5 minutes or until heated through. Reduce heat to low, cover and simmer for 10 minutes or until vegetables are soft.

2. Stir in chickpeas and tofu. Increase heat to medium and cook until the mixture begins to bubble. Reduce heat to low, cover and simmer for 10 minutes or until flavors are blended.

3. Stir in soy milk, coconut, sugar and salt and pepper to taste. Simmer, uncovered, for 5 minutes.

Variations

For a slightly deeper flavor, add ½ tsp (2 mL) turmeric along with the ginger. If you like a bit of heat, add 3 or 4 drops of hot sesame oil.

Sprinkle the top of each portion with 2 tbsp (25 mL) finely chopped peanuts.

Tasty Chickpea Cakes

We love this version of the Middle Eastern specialty falafel. The combination of seasoning and oatmeal, which can't be detected in the final result, make this a satisfying main dish.

Tips

In some locations, chickpeas are known as garbanzo beans.

If you prefer, use 2 tbsp (25 mL) chopped fresh mint leaves in place of the dried.

❧ *Food processor*

½ cup	rolled oats (quick-cooking or old-fashioned)	125 mL
1 tbsp	freshly squeezed lemon juice	15 mL
1	can (14 to 19 oz/398 to 540 mL) chickpeas, drained and rinsed (see Tips, left), or 1 cup (250 mL) dried chickpeas, soaked, cooked and drained	1
2 tbsp	coarsely chopped Italian parsley	25 mL
1	small onion, coarsely chopped	1
3	cloves garlic, minced (1 tbsp/15 mL)	3
2 tsp	cumin seeds	10 mL
2 tsp	dried mint leaves (see Tips, left)	10 mL
1 tsp	chili powder	5 mL
½ tsp	salt	2 mL
¼ tsp	freshly ground black pepper	1 mL
¼ cup	olive or vegetable oil	50 mL
3 tbsp	cornmeal or bread crumbs	45 mL

1. In food processor, combine oats with lemon juice and pulse three or four times or until blended. Add chickpeas and parsley and pulse 10 times or until chickpeas are ground and mixture is blended but not puréed.

2. Add onion, garlic, cumin seeds, mint, chili powder, salt and pepper. Pulse 5 times or until mixed. (The large pieces of onion and the chickpeas should be broken down, but the mixture should have a coarse texture.)

3. With moistened hands, shape mixture into five cakes, each about 2½ inches (6.25 cm) in diameter and ¾ inch (2 cm) thick. Sprinkle cornmeal on both sides.

4. In a large skillet, heat oil over high heat until hot but not smoking. Add cakes and fry for 1 minute. Reduce heat to medium and fry for 1 to 2 minutes longer or until browned. Flip cakes and fry for 2 to 3 minutes longer or until browned

Variations

Substitute sesame seeds for the cumin seeds.

Add a splash of sesame oil to the vegetable oil when frying the cakes.

This tasty tofu can be eaten as a snack, as an appetizer or in an Asian stir-fry. It can be served hot or cold.

Tips

To drain tofu, place the cubes on a plate lined with a double layer of paper towels. Cover with another paper towel and another plate and place a weight on top of the plate to press the water from the tofu. Let stand for 30 minutes. Drain off water.

Although tofu is a staple in the vegan diet, it can be high in fat. If you're concerned about fat intake, look for lower-fat versions, which work well in both this dish and Italian-Style Baked Tofu (see recipe, page 102).

Asian-Style Baked Tofu

❧ *Preheat oven to 350°F (180°C)*
❧ *8-inch (2 L) square glass baking dish*

¼ cup	low-sodium soy sauce	50 mL
¼ cup	vegan teriyaki sauce	50 mL
2 tbsp	freshly squeezed lime juice	25 mL
1 tbsp	finely grated gingerroot	15 mL
2	cloves garlic, minced (about 2 tsp/10 mL)	2
1 lb	firm or extra-firm tofu, cut in 1-inch (2.5 cm) cubes and drained (see Tips, left)	500 g

1. In a small bowl, whisk together soy sauce, teriyaki sauce, lime juice, ginger and garlic.
2. Arrange tofu evenly over the bottom of baking dish. Add sauce and stir until cubes are completely covered with sauce. Marinate for 1 hour at room temperature or in the refrigerator for at least 2 hours or for up to 8 hours.
3. Bake, uncovered, in preheated oven, for 35 to 40 minutes, stirring and turning pieces over after 20 minutes, or until tofu is firm and liquid is absorbed.

Italian-Style Baked Tofu

Like Asian-Style Baked Tofu (see recipe, page 101), this recipe is versatile. Serve it as an appetizer, in salads, or crumbled and used as a cheese substitute in Italian dishes. You can also use this to make a sauce (see Variation, below) for pasta or potatoes.

Tip

To drain tofu, place the cubes on a plate lined with a double layer of paper towels. Cover with another paper towel, then another plate. Place a weight on top of the plate to press the water out of the tofu. Let stand for 30 minutes. Drain off water.

❧ *Preheat oven to 350°F (180°C)*
❧ *8-inch (2 L) square glass baking dish*

1 lb	firm or extra-firm tofu, cut in 1-inch (2.5 cm) cubes and drained (see Tips, left)	500 g
2	cloves garlic, minced (about 2 tsp/10 mL)	2
1 tsp	dried oregano leaves	5 mL
1 tsp	dried basil leaves	5 mL
¼ tsp	salt, or to taste	1 mL
	Freshly ground black pepper	
¼ cup	prepared Italian salad dressing	50 mL

1. In baking dish, combine tofu, garlic, oregano, basil and salt and pepper to taste. Drizzle with dressing, then stir until tofu is evenly coated. Marinate for 1 hour at room temperature or in the refrigerator for at least 2 hours or for up to 8 hours.

2. Bake, uncovered, in preheated oven, for 35 to 40 minutes, stirring and turning pieces over after 20 minutes, or until tofu is firm and liquid is absorbed.

Variation

Before baking, add 1 can (14 oz/398 mL) seasoned diced tomatoes to tofu and mix well. Serve over pasta.

For the Kids

The cornmeal in the batter gives a nice texture and taste to these waffles. Blueberry maple syrup tops them off nicely.

Tips

We've used regular all-purpose flour in this recipe because it is the kind people are most likely to have on hand. If you prefer the unbleached version, by all means use it.

Substitute whole wheat or buckwheat flour for 1 cup (250 mL) of the all-purpose flour.

Cornmeal Waffles with Blueberry Maple Syrup

❧ *Preheat oven to 200°F (100°C)*
❧ *Waffle iron, preheated*

WAFFLES

3 cups	all-purpose flour (see Tips, left)	750 mL
3 tbsp	cornmeal	45 mL
1 tsp	salt	5 mL
1 tsp	baking soda	5 mL
	Egg replacer for 3 eggs, prepared according to package directions	
3 cups	vanilla-flavor rice milk or soy milk	750 mL
6 tbsp	soy margarine, melted	90 mL
1 tsp	distilled white vinegar	5 mL

SYRUP

1 1/2 cups	blueberries	375 mL
1 cup	pure maple syrup	250 mL
2 tbsp	freshly squeezed lemon juice	25 mL

1. *Waffles:* In a large bowl, mix together flour, cornmeal, salt and baking soda.

2. In a separate bowl, whisk together egg replacer, rice milk, soy margarine and vinegar.

3. Using a wooden spoon, make a well in the middle of the dry mixture. Fill with the rice milk mixture. Stir just until blended. (Don't worry about lumps.) Ladle enough batter into the waffle iron to cover about two-thirds of the cooking surface. Close lid and cook for 4 to 5 minutes or until the lid lifts easily. If it sticks or the waffle begins to tear, close the lid and continue cooking for 1 minute longer. Using a fork, remove waffle. Place on a baking sheet and keep warm in preheated oven. Repeat with remaining batter.

4. *Syrup:* Meanwhile, in a saucepan over medium-high heat, combine blueberries, syrup and lemon juice and bring to a boil. Remove from heat and transfer to a syrup pitcher. Serve over hot waffles.

Variation

Use thawed frozen blueberries instead of fresh blueberries. Pour off their juices before combining with the syrup.

Luscious Apple Butter

This delicious old-fashioned spread has lots of appeal. Serve it on toast for breakfast, on nut butter sandwiches for lunch or as a snack or dessert topping. You can also forgo the puréeing and serve a warm, chunky version as an accompaniment to puddings or vanilla-flavor soy yogurt. Usually apple butter is slowly simmered on the stove, but this baked version makes it a less-fussy preparation.

Tips

There are many varieties of molasses, which differ in flavor. Try a few to see which ones suit your taste. Although blackstrap molasses is a good source of iron, it has a strong flavor and can be overly assertive for seasoning apples. We prefer fancy molasses from the supermarket in this recipe.

This recipe can be doubled and baked in a larger pan.

A dollop of apple butter is delicious on top of Phyllo Cups (see recipe, page 173) filled with vanilla-flavor soy yogurt. If you prefer, add a garnish of sautéed apple slices.

❦ Preheat oven to 400°F (200°C)
❦ 13-by 9-inch (3 L) baking dish, ungreased
❦ Food processor or blender

¼ cup	water	50 mL
10	small to medium cooking apples (such as McIntosh), peeled, cored and thinly sliced	10
⅓ cup	packed dark brown sugar or other dry sweetener	75 mL
¼ tsp	ground cinnamon	1 mL
¼ tsp	ground cloves	1 mL
⅛ tsp	ground allspice	0.5 mL
Pinch	ground nutmeg	Pinch
3 tbsp	molasses (see Tips, left)	45 mL
1 tbsp	freshly squeezed lemon juice	15 mL

1. Pour water into baking dish. Add apples and brown sugar. Stir until sugar is dissolved. Sprinkle cinnamon, cloves, allspice and nutmeg over top and mix well.

2. Drizzle molasses and lemon juice over top. Stir well.

3. Bake, uncovered, in preheated oven, stirring every 20 minutes, for 1 hour or until apples are deep brown, soft and coated with syrup. Let cool in baking dish on a rack for 5 to 10 minutes.

4. Transfer cooled apple mixture to a food processor or blender and purée until smooth. Store in a glass jar or airtight container in the refrigerator for up to 6 weeks.

Variation

For convenience, make this recipe using one 26-oz (700 mL) jar unsweetened applesauce instead of the apples. Omit the water and bake at 375°F (190°C) for 1 hour. No puréeing is needed.

Berry Smoothies

Berry smoothies have become popular breakfast foods and snacks for many families. And for good reason: kids love the taste and can design their own smoothies, and parents can feel good about giving these nutritious drinks to their children any time of day.

Tips

This mixture will be very thick. If you like thinner smoothies, add juice and blend to the desired consistency.

It may be necessary to stop the blender, scrape down the side of the jug with a rubber spatula, then blend again to get a smooth, even texture.

To make it easier to blend the ingredients, run frozen berries under warm water to soften before blending. They should be frozen on the inside but soft on the outside so they chill the solution but blend easily.

✨ Blender

1 cup	frozen unsweetened raspberries	250 mL
1 cup	frozen unsweetened strawberries	250 mL
1 cup	vanilla-flavor soy milk	250 mL
¼ cup	silken tofu (about 2 oz/60 g)	50 mL
1 tbsp	granulated natural cane sugar, or to taste	15 mL
	Cranberry or other fruit juice, optional (see Tips, left)	

1. In blender, combine raspberries, strawberries, soy milk and silken tofu. Blend on high speed until thick and smooth.
2. Add sugar to taste, and juice, if using, and blend on high speed for another 15 to 20 seconds.

Variations

Add half a banana, sliced; replace one of the berries with blueberries; or replace the silken tofu with ¼ cup (50 mL) soy ice cream.

You can easily vary the amounts of ingredients to suit your taste. Maxine's 12-year-old daughter, Jennifer, loves the consistency of this smoothie, but her 21-year-old stepdaughter, Elizabeth, prefers less tofu and more fruit and sugar. Experiment to find your favorite combination.

Almond Butter

This nut butter has versatility and an underlying sweetness that makes it deserving of a regular spot in your refrigerator. It makes a great breakfast spread on whole wheat toast with pieces of soft date. It is a welcome change from peanut butter in nutritious sandwiches and can be served on apple wedges as a snack between meals. It is delicious stuffed in dried fruits, such as dates, prunes or apricots.

Tips

To see if almonds are properly toasted, carefully break or cut one almond in half. It should be light golden brown on the inside.

Almonds vary in moisture content, depending on how fresh they are. That's why there is a range in the amount of oil required to make the butter smooth.

Preheat oven to 350°F (180°C)
Rimmed baking sheet, ungreased
Food processor

2 cups	whole raw almonds	500 mL
4 to 6 tbsp	vegetable oil	50 to 90 mL
Pinch	salt, optional	Pinch

1. On baking sheet, spread almonds in a single layer. Bake in preheated oven for 12 to 14 minutes or until toasted and fragrant.

2. Transfer to food processor. Pulse until almonds are evenly chopped, occasionally stopping and scraping down the side of the bowl. Add 2 tbsp (25 mL) of the vegetable oil, and salt, if using. Process for 1 minute. Remove lid and scrape down the side of the bowl with a rubber spatula. Replace lid and, with motor running, slowly add remaining oil, 1 tbsp (15 mL) at a time, down the feeder tube, processing until mixture is smooth and spreadable.

3. Transfer to a glass jar or airtight container and refrigerate for up to 1 month.

Variation

Add 1 tbsp (15 mL) dry sweetener (such as granulated natural cane sugar or sucanat) and $\frac{1}{2}$ tsp (2 mL) almond extract for a sweet almond butter.

Banana and Almond Butter Whole Wheat Pita Pockets

2	whole wheat pitas (8 inches/20 cm), cut in half	2
1/2 cup	Almond Butter (see recipe, page 107)	125 mL
4	bananas, cut into 1/4-inch (0.5 cm) slices	4

1. Gently separate the sides of the pocket of each pita half, keeping the edge attached. Spread 2 tbsp (25 mL) almond butter over the inside bottom of each pocket, then cover with sliced bananas.

Variations

Replace almond butter with other nut butters, such as peanut butter (so long as your child is not going anywhere where peanut allergies are a concern).

Substitute 8 slices whole wheat bread for the pita bread.

Spicy Black Bean Quesadillas

Tip

If you don't have garlic-infused oil, make your own for use in this recipe. In a small skillet, heat ½ tsp (2 mL) garlic powder with 2 tbsp (25 mL) olive oil over medium–low heat for 30 seconds. Use immediately, as it's dangerous to keep homemade garlic oil because of the risk of botulism. Commercial varieties have additives that prevent this.

1 cup	Spicy Black Bean Dip (see recipe, page 33)	250 mL
8	8-inch (20 cm) corn tortillas	8
½ cup	shredded vegan Cheddar cheese alternative	125 mL
2 tbsp	garlic-infused oil (see Tip, left)	25 mL

1. Spread black bean dip evenly over four of the tortillas. Sprinkle each with vegan Cheddar cheese alternative and cover with another tortilla. Using a pastry brush, brush both sides of each quesadilla with oil.

2. In a nonstick skillet sprayed with olive oil cooking spray, over medium heat, cook quesadillas, one at a time, for 1 minute or until crisp, checking often to prevent burning. Flip over and cook for 1 minute on other side or until crisp. Transfer to a cutting board and cut into quarters.

Variations

Sprinkle each quesadilla with 1 tbsp (15 mL) chopped fresh cilantro leaves before topping with the second tortilla.

Replace the corn tortillas with your tortilla of choice. There are many flavors available, and all would work well in this recipe.

Here's a healthier version of French fries that parents can feel comfortable serving their children.

Baked French Fries

❧ *Preheat oven to 425°F (220°C)*
❧ *Large rimmed baking sheet, lined with foil*

5	medium baking potatoes (unpeeled)	5
2 tbsp	olive oil	25 mL
1	clove garlic, minced (about 1 tsp/5 mL)	1
1/2 tsp	salt	2 mL
1/2 tsp	freshly ground black pepper	2 mL

1. Gently scrub potatoes under running water. Cut each potato lengthwise into 1/4- to 1/2-inch (0.5 to 1 cm) thick slices. Cut each slice into two or three strips. Each strip should be about 3 inches (7.5 cm) long and 1/4 inch (0.5 cm) wide.

2. In a small bowl, combine olive oil, garlic, salt and pepper.

3. Arrange potato strips in a single layer on prepared baking sheet. Using a pastry brush, brush potatoes with olive oil mixture on all sides.

4. Bake in preheated oven, turning every 10 to 12 minutes, for 40 to 45 minutes or until brown and crisp on all sides.

Variation

For kids with adventurous palates, try adding a pinch of cayenne pepper to the olive oil mixture.

Granola Bars

These are the perfect fix for breakfast on the run, after-school snacks or late-night munching for big and little kids!

Tips

Chopping the raisins very finely releases natural sugars, which are used as the binder in this recipe. Use a sharp knife and chop a few spoonfuls at a time, chopping them into flecks that are roughly one-eighth the size of a raisin or until they clump together when squeezed. Using a butter knife, scrape the sharp knife blade clean periodically while chopping.

We use raw almonds in this recipe, but you can use blanched if you prefer.

Preheat oven to 325°F (160°C)
Rimmed baking sheet, lined with foil

3 cups	quick-cooking rolled oats	750 mL
1 cup	dark raisins, finely chopped (see Tips, left)	250 mL
½ cup	almonds, coarsely chopped (see Tips, left)	125 mL
1 tsp	ground cinnamon	5 mL
¾ tsp	salt	4 mL
½ cup	pure maple syrup	125 mL
¼ cup	water or apple juice	50 mL
2 tbsp	packed brown sugar or other dry sweetener	25 mL
1 tsp	vanilla	5 mL

1. In a large bowl, mix together oats, raisins, almonds, cinnamon and salt.

2. In a small saucepan, combine maple syrup, water and brown sugar. Bring to a boil over medium–high heat, stirring, until sugar is dissolved. Remove from heat and stir in vanilla. Drizzle over oat mixture and stir until evenly moistened.

3. With moistened hands, divide mixture into 10 equal portions. Squeeze each into a cylinder about 4 inches (10 cm) long. Place, 2 to 3 inches (5 to 7.5 cm) apart, on prepared baking sheet. Using the side of a wide knife or a spatula, flatten into neat 1¾-inch (4.5 cm) wide and ½-inch (1 cm) thick bars. Use the knife to press the sides and corners into straight, uniform edges. Bake in preheated oven for 25 to 30 minutes or until light brown and fragrant. Let cool in pan on a rack for 5 to 10 minutes. Transfer to rack and let cool completely. Store in an airtight container for up to 1 week.

Variations

Use old-fashioned rolled oats in place of the quick-cooking. Because they are drier than the quick-cooking version, add extra maple syrup and water (1 tbsp/15 mL each). After combining the granola mixture with the syrup, transfer to a food processor and pulse six to eight times to help the ingredients bind together. Continue with Step 3.

Replace the almonds with other chopped nuts or whole seeds, such as walnuts, hazelnuts or pumpkin seeds.

Nutty Fruit Balls

These snack treats came about when Beth's friend Pattie, a corporate chef, decided to remove refined sugar from her diet and began improvising with new and different combinations. This recipe is Beth's idea of a healthy alternative to chocolate truffles. It makes a great pick-me-up any time of day.

Tips

Medjool dates are ideal for this recipe. They can be found in natural foods markets and some large grocery stores. If using this type of date, it is not necessary to soften them in boiling water.

These balls can also be frozen in an airtight container for up to 6 weeks. Thaw before serving.

12 oz	small firm fresh dates (see Tips, left), about 1 1/2 cups/375 mL	375 g
2 cups	boiling water	500 mL
1 1/4 cups	coarsely chopped walnuts, divided	300 mL
1/2 cup	dried apricots, cut in 1/4-inch (0.5 cm) pieces	125 mL
1/4 cup	golden or dark raisins	50 mL
1/4 cup	dried cranberries	50 mL
1/2 tsp	finely grated orange zest	2 mL
2 tbsp	freshly squeezed orange juice	25 mL
1/4 tsp	ground allspice	1 mL
2 tbsp	dry bread crumbs	25 mL

1. Using a paring knife, cut along the length of each date and pop out the pit. In a heatproof bowl, combine dates with boiling water and steep for 1 minute. Drain. Using a fork, press dates against the side of the bowl until a paste forms. Set aside.

2. In a small mixing bowl, combine 1/2 cup (125 mL) walnuts, apricots, raisins, cranberries, orange zest and juice and allspice. Add fruit mixture to date paste and mix well.

3. Finely chop remaining 3/4 cup (175 mL) walnuts. In a small bowl, mix walnuts with bread crumbs.

4. With moistened hands, roll fruit mixture into 1-inch (2.5 cm) balls. Roll each ball in the bread-crumb mixture until completely coated. Refrigerate in an airtight container for up to 2 weeks (see Tips, left).

Variations

Use 1/2 cup (125 mL) dried cherries instead of the cranberries and raisins. You can also substitute chopped pecans for the walnuts.

Replace bread crumbs with an equal amount of unsweetened or sweetened shredded coconut.

Replace orange zest with lemon zest and orange juice with 1 tbsp (15 mL) lemon juice and 1 tbsp (15 mL) water.

Cheeseless Pizza

This customized pizza is healthy and tasty, plus it can become a family project, with all family members designing their own portions of the pizza. In Maxine's family, the kids roll out the pizza dough while the adults prepare the toppings. They choose the tomato sauce together, then each person decides what to put on his or her portion of the pizza.

Tip

Use prepared tomato sauce in this recipe or make your own (see recipe, page 154).

❧ Preheat oven to 450°F (230°C)
❧ 17-by 11-inch (42.5 by 27.5 cm) rimmed baking sheet or 16-inch (40 cm) round pizza pan, greased

1 lb	prepared pizza dough	500 g
3 cups	tomato sauce (see Tip, left)	750 mL
1	jar (6 oz/175 g) marinated artichoke hearts, drained and quartered	1
1 cup	black olives, pitted and halved	250 mL
3	roasted red bell peppers (see Roasted Bell Peppers, page 151), skin removed and sliced into 1/2-inch (1 cm) strips	3

CARAMELIZED ONIONS

3 tbsp	olive oil, divided	45 mL
2	medium sweet onions (such as Vidalia), cut into 1/4-inch (0.5 cm) slices (about 2 cups/500 mL)	2

1. *Caramelized Onions:* In a large skillet, heat 2 tbsp (25 mL) olive oil over medium-high heat until very hot but not smoking. Add sliced onions and drizzle with remaining 1 tbsp (15 mL) oil. Reduce heat to low, cover and cook, stirring every 10 minutes to prevent burning and sticking, for 25 to 30 minutes or until onions are soft and brown.

2. Meanwhile, on prepared baking sheet, spread dough using your fingertips to gently press the dough out so it covers the entire sheet. Bake in preheated oven for 6 to 8 minutes or until dough starts to harden but not brown. Let cool in pan on a rack for about 10 minutes.

3. Spread tomato sauce over crust and scatter caramelized onions, artichokes, olives and roasted peppers over top. Bake for 10 to 12 minutes or until crust is browned around the edges.

Variation

Fresh herbs add excitement to your pizza. Try sprinkling the onions with 1 tbsp (15 mL) finely chopped fresh basil, oregano, parsley, and/or garlic chives.

Sloppy Joes

Tips

It's necessary to stir the bean mixture during cooking to ensure that the soy meat alternative doesn't burn.

This makes a good leftover and may be even better the second day. Refrigerate in an airtight container for up to 3 days.

2 tbsp	vegetable oil	25 mL
1	onion, finely chopped	1
1	green bell pepper, finely chopped	1
8 oz	soy ground meat alternative	250 g
1	can (14 to 19 oz/398 to 540 mL) pinto or red kidney beans, drained and rinsed, or 1 cup (250 mL) dried pinto or red kidney beans, soaked, cooked and drained (see Legumes, page 13)	1
½ cup	ketchup	125 mL
½ cup	chili sauce	125 mL
1 tbsp	Dijon mustard	15 mL
1 tbsp	distilled white vinegar	15 mL
1 tsp	granulated natural cane sugar or other dry sweetener	5 mL
	Salt	

1. In a large nonstick skillet, heat oil over medium heat for 1 minute. Add onion and green pepper and cook, stirring frequently, for 4 to 6 minutes or until onion is soft and green peppers are tender.

2. Add soy ground meat alternative and cook, stirring, for 3 minutes. Stir in pinto beans and reduce heat to low. Cook, stirring, for 3 minutes or until heated through.

3. In a small bowl, combine ketchup, chili sauce, mustard, vinegar, sugar and salt to taste. Add sauce to skillet and stir well. Simmer, uncovered, for 3 to 4 minutes or until hot.

Variations

If you like a spicier version, add hot pepper sauce to taste after the cooking is completed.

Use a red, orange or yellow bell pepper in place of the green.

American Chop Soy

This vegan version of an American classic is easy to make as well as delicious. Served with salad, it makes a perfect nutritious comfort meal.

Tip

Some canned diced tomatoes come with a variety of seasonings, such as Italian herbs or roasted garlic and basil. Any work well in this recipe.

6 oz	elbow macaroni	175 g
2 tbsp	vegetable oil	25 mL
1	large onion, coarsely chopped (about 2 cups/500 mL)	1
8 oz	mushrooms, sliced (about 2 cups/500 mL)	250 g
8 oz	soy ground meat alternative	250 g
1	can (14 oz/398 mL) diced tomatoes, with juices (see Tip, left)	1
¼ cup	ketchup	50 mL
Dash	hot pepper sauce	Dash
	Salt and freshly ground black pepper	

1. In a large pot of boiling salted water, cook macaroni for 7 minutes or according to package directions, until tender to the bite. Drain.

2. Meanwhile, in a large nonstick skillet, heat oil over medium heat. Add onion and cook, stirring, for 3 minutes or until softened. Add mushrooms and cook, stirring, for 2 minutes. Stir in soy meat alternative and cook, stirring, for 3 minutes.

3. In a bowl, combine diced tomatoes, ketchup and hot pepper sauce. Stir into skillet, reduce heat to low and cook, uncovered, for 5 minutes or until heated through. Stir in drained pasta and mix well.

Make-Your-Own Tacos

Tip

Use prepared salsa or Tomato and Garlic Salsa (see recipe, page 29) in this recipe.

FILLING

1 tbsp	vegetable oil	15 mL
1	medium sweet onion (such as Vidalia), finely chopped	1
12 oz	soy ground meat alternative	375 g
1 1/2 cups	salsa (see Tip, left)	375 mL

TOPPINGS

2 cups	shredded vegan Cheddar cheese alternative	500 mL
1 1/2 cups	shredded lettuce	375 mL
1 cup	canned or cooked black beans or red kidney beans, drained and rinsed	250 mL
1	sweet onion (such as Vidalia), finely chopped	1
1 cup	pitted black olives, sliced	250 mL
1 cup	chopped seeded tomatoes	250 mL
1/2 cup	salsa	125 mL
1/2 cup	chopped fresh cilantro leaves, optional	125 mL
12	taco shells	12

1. *Filling:* In a large nonstick skillet, heat oil over medium heat for 30 seconds. Add onion and cook, stirring, for 3 minutes or until softened. Add soy meat alternative and reduce heat to low. Cook, stirring, for 3 to 4 minutes or until heated through. Stir in salsa, mixing well. Cover and simmer for 5 minutes or until flavors are blended. Transfer to serving bowl.

2. *Toppings:* In separate small bowls, set out vegan Cheddar cheese alternative, lettuce, beans, onion, olives, tomatoes, salsa and cilantro, if using. Each person fills his or her own taco shells with filling and toppings.

Variation

Add Chunky Guacamole (see recipe, page 28), pinto beans, refried beans, chopped jalapeño peppers, vegan sour cream alternative or any other accompaniments you prefer.

This pancake works well as a main course, served with salad or another vegetable, or as a side dish to vegetable stew or a tofu dish.

Tips

If the pancake starts to burn over medium–high heat, reduce heat to medium and increase cooking time.

Serve these pancakes with ketchup, applesauce or vegan sour cream alternative.

Potato Pancake with Soy Sausage and Onion

❧ *Preheat oven to 250°F (120°C)*

2 tbsp	soy margarine	25 mL
1	onion, coarsely chopped	1
2	baking potatoes, peeled and shredded	2
1/2 tsp	garlic powder	2 mL
1/4 tsp	salt, or to taste	1 mL
1/4 tsp	freshly ground black pepper, or to taste	1 mL
1	Italian-flavored soy sausage, chopped	1
2 tsp	olive oil, divided	10 mL

1. In a small nonstick skillet, heat margarine over medium heat for 30 seconds. Add onion and cook, stirring, for 3 minutes or until softened. Transfer onion to a bowl and set skillet aside.

2. Add potatoes, garlic powder, salt, pepper and soy sausage to onion and mix well.

3. Return skillet to medium-high heat. Heat 1 tsp (5 mL) of olive oil for 1 minute, swirling the skillet to coat the bottom with oil. Add half of the potato mixture, pushing down firmly with a spatula until you hear the mixture sizzle (see Tips, left). Cook, pressing often, for 3 to 5 minutes or until bottom is browned and crisp. Place a plate or small baking sheet over the skillet and flip pancake onto plate. Carefully slide the pancake, uncooked side down, off the plate and back into the skillet. Cook, pressing often, for 3 to 5 minutes or until browned and crisp. Carefully slide pancake onto an ovenproof plate, guiding it with the spatula. Keep warm in preheated oven. Repeat with remaining oil and potato mixture.

Variation

Add 1 tbsp (15 mL) chopped fresh chives or your favorite herb to the potato mixture.

Crispy Cinnamon Roll-Ups

Tip

Some vegan cream cheese alternatives have stronger flavors than others. We prefer a mild vegan cream cheese alternative for this recipe.

Preheat oven to 375°F (190°C)
Rimmed baking sheet, greased
Rolling pin

3 tbsp	granulated natural cane sugar	45 mL
½ tsp	ground cinnamon	2 mL
10	slices whole-grain or white bread, crusts removed	10
3 oz	vegan cream cheese–style spread (about ¼ cup/50 mL)	90 g
3 oz	vegan butter alternative spread (about ¼ cup/50 mL)	90 g

1. In a small container, combine sugar with cinnamon. Pour onto a plate.

2. With rolling pin, flatten each slice of bread, rolling in both directions. Spread a thin layer of vegan cream cheese on each slice of flattened bread.

3. If the bread is rectangular, position with the long side facing you. Tightly roll the bread away from you into a cylinder, jelly roll–style.

4. Spread butter alternative on the outside of each roll, then roll in the cinnamon mixture until covered. Cut each roll into three pieces and place, 1½ inches (4 cm) apart, on prepared baking sheet. Bake in preheated oven for 10 to 12 minutes or until crisp. Serve immediately.

Variation

Instead of spreading the bread with vegan cream cheese alternative, make your own spread as follows: In a small nonstick skillet over medium heat, melt 2 tbsp (25 mL) soy margarine. Reduce heat to medium–low and add 2 tbsp (25 mL) corn syrup and 2 tsp (10 mL) unsweetened cocoa powder, stirring continuously until blended. Remove from heat. Use a pastry brush to spread chocolate mixture on bread, then follow steps 3 through 5.

Lemon Snow Cones

This is a classic kid-friendly treat. It is very easy to make and has a refreshing zing. By using an ice cream scoop to mound it in a small paper cup, you create a homemade snow cone that looks just like the real thing.

Tip

Be sure the mixture is firm before scraping it in order to get the best consistency for snow cones. If it is not firm enough, return to the freezer.

4 or 5 small paper cups or small bowls

1 1/2 cups	water	375 mL
3/4 cup	granulated natural cane sugar or other dry sweetener	175 mL
2 tsp	finely grated lemon zest	10 mL
1/2 cup	freshly squeezed lemon juice	125 mL

1. In a small pot, combine water, sugar and lemon zest and bring to a boil over high heat, stirring, until sugar is dissolved and a thick syrup forms. Remove from heat and stir in lemon juice.

2. Pour into a shallow freezer-safe container and freeze, uncovered, for 3 hours or until frozen solid.

3. Using the tines of a fork, scrape the frozen lemon mixture until it has all been shaved into granules. Using an ice cream scoop, scrape ice into a ball and place in paper cups or small bowls. Serve immediately.

Variation

In place of lemon zest and juice, substitute equal amounts of lime zest and juice.

Chocolate Pudding

Tips

If you prefer, substitute 3 tbsp (45 mL) arrowroot for the cornstarch.

Constant whisking while cooking ensures that the pudding thickens evenly without lumps and doesn't scorch.

This recipe can easily be doubled with excellent results.

For a lower-fat version of the pudding, use a low-fat dairy-free beverage. For a richer consistency and taste, you can use beverages with higher fat contents.

1/4 cup	unsweetened cocoa powder	50 mL
2 1/2 tbsp	cornstarch (see Tips, left)	32 mL
1/3 cup	granulated natural cane sugar or other dry sweetener	75 mL
Pinch	salt	Pinch
2 cups	plain rice milk or soy milk	500 mL
2 tbsp	vegan chocolate chips, optional	25 mL
1/2 tsp	vanilla	2 mL

1. Sift cocoa and cornstarch together into a pot. Whisk in sugar and salt.

2. Gradually whisk in about half of the rice milk, whisking constantly to prevent lumps from forming. Pour in remaining rice milk, whisking well.

3. Bring to a boil over medium–high heat, whisking constantly. As soon as pudding reaches a boil, remove from heat and whisk, adding chocolate chips, if using, and vanilla, until chips are melted and blended.

4. Transfer to four pudding cups or bowls and refrigerate for 1 hour or until thoroughly chilled and set.

Pastas and Grains

Pasta Puttanesca

*Easy and filling, this is the
perfect recipe when everyone's
hungry and you don't have
a lot of time to cook an
elaborate meal. Add capers
and accompany with a bowl
of vegan Parmesan cheese
alternative to serve company.*

Tips

Use canned tomatoes with
or without seasoning, as
you prefer.

Many varieties of black
olives work well in this
sauce. Try oil-cured,
Moroccan or kalamata
olives for best results.

1 tbsp	olive oil	15 mL
2	onions, coarsely chopped	2
3	cloves garlic, minced (about 1 tbsp/15 mL)	3
1	can (28 oz/796 mL) diced tomatoes, with juices (see Tip, left)	1
3 tbsp	tomato paste	45 mL
2 tbsp	dry red wine	25 mL
1 cup	pitted oil-cured black olives, halved (see Tips, left)	250 mL
¼ cup	chopped drained oil-packed sun-dried tomatoes	50 mL
2 tsp	dried basil leaves	10 mL
2 tsp	dried oregano leaves	10 mL
½ tsp	hot pepper flakes, or to taste	2 mL
½ to 1 tsp	granulated natural cane sugar	2 to 5 mL
8 oz	penne or other short pasta	250 g

1. In a large nonstick skillet, heat oil over medium heat for 30 seconds. Add onions and garlic and cook, stirring, for 3 minutes or until onion is softened. Stir in tomatoes, tomato paste and red wine and bring to a boil.

2. Reduce heat to low and stir in olives, sun-dried tomatoes, basil, oregano and hot pepper flakes. Taste and add sugar, a little at a time, as necessary, to smooth any bitterness. Simmer, uncovered, for 10 minutes or until thickened.

3. Meanwhile, in large pot of boiling salted water, cook pasta for 8 minutes or until tender to the bite, or according to package instructions. Drain. Serve sauce over hot pasta.

Variations

For a heartier meal, slice 2 Italian-style soy sausages and add along with the wine.

Add 2 tbsp (25 mL) drained capers along with the sun-dried tomatoes.

Stuffed Shells

Stuffed shells are a classic. Here's our family-friendly vegan version, which is hearty, healthy and simple to make.

Tips

Make sure that the shells are not overcooked. If they are too soft, they will break when stuffed. To make sure they are well drained, place, open side down, on a paper towel–lined plate while preparing stuffing.

Use prepared tomato sauce or make your own (see recipe, page 154).

❧ *Preheat oven to 350°F (180°C)*
❧ *13-by 9 inch (3 L) baking dish, greased*

8 oz	large pasta shells (about 18)	250 g
10 oz	vegan veggie burger patties (about 4), thawed if frozen	300 g
¾ cup	dry bread crumbs	175 mL
3 tbsp	chopped fresh oregano leaves (or 1 tbsp/15 mL dried)	45 mL
1 tbsp	garlic powder	15 mL
	Salt, optional	
2 tbsp	vegetable oil	25 mL
1	large onion, coarsely chopped (about 2 cups/500 mL)	1
1	can (14 oz/398 mL) diced tomatoes, with juices	1
2 cups	tomato sauce (see Tips, left)	500 mL

1. In a large pot of boiling salted water, cook pasta shells for 12 minutes or according to package instructions, until just tender to the bite. Drain well and let cool (see Tips, left).

2. In a bowl, using a fork, crumble veggie patties. Add bread crumbs, oregano, garlic powder and salt to taste, if using, and mix.

3. In a large nonstick skillet, heat oil over medium heat for 30 seconds. Add onion and cook, stirring, for 3 minutes or until softened. Add burger mixture and stir well. Stir in diced tomatoes, reduce heat to low and cook, stirring occasionally, for 5 minutes or until flavors are blended.

4. Using a small spoon, stuff shells with vegetable mixture, packing tightly. Place in prepared baking dish, open side up. Cover with tomato sauce. Bake, uncovered, in preheated oven for 25 minutes or until sauce is bubbling and shells are hot in the center.

Variation

Sprinkle shredded vegan Cheddar or mozzarella cheese alternative over each shell before baking, if desired.

Pad Thai

This dish, which is a kind of catchall in its native Thailand, can be very adaptable. Feel free to customize this recipe with your favorite seasonal vegetables. It makes a nice main course or you can serve smaller portions as a first course.

Tips

In many locations, green onions are known as scallions.

To soften noodles, make sure the water is scalding (too hot to touch but not boiling).

6 oz	silken tofu, cut into ½-inch (1 cm) cubes	175 g
1 tbsp	vegetable oil	15 mL
1	red bell pepper, cut in thin 2-inch (5 cm) long strips	1
1	carrot, shredded into long shreds or cut into thin rounds	1
4 oz	bean sprouts	125 g
¾ cup	salted roasted peanuts, coarsely chopped	175 mL
2 tbsp	chopped fresh cilantro leaves, optional	25 mL

NOODLES

8 oz	wide rice noodles	250 g
6 cups	scalding hot water (see Tips, left)	1.5 L

DRESSING

⅓ cup	seasoned rice vinegar	75 mL
¼ cup	granulated natural cane sugar or other dry sweetener	50 mL
2 tbsp	finely chopped fresh basil leaves, divided	25 mL
2	cloves garlic, minced (about 2 tsp/10 mL)	2
3	green onions, thinly sliced, white and green parts separated, divided (see Tips, left)	3
¾ tsp	Asian chili paste (or ½ tsp/2 mL hot pepper flakes)	4 mL
½ tsp	salt	2 mL
2 tbsp	sesame oil	25 mL
1 tbsp	vegetable oil	15 mL

1. *Noodles:* In a heatproof bowl, soak noodles in hot water for about 20 minutes or until softened, or prepare according to package directions. Drain.
2. Meanwhile, on a plate lined with a double layer of paper towels, arrange tofu cubes. Let stand for 15 minutes to absorb moisture.

3. *Dressing:* In a bowl, combine vinegar with sugar. Stir until sugar is dissolved. Add 1 tbsp (15 mL) basil, garlic, white part of green onions, chili paste and salt. Whisk in sesame oil and vegetable oil until well blended. Set aside.

4. In a large skillet, heat oil over medium heat for 1 minute or until hot but not smoking. Add red pepper and carrot and cook, stirring, for 2 to 3 minutes or until almost tender. Add tofu and half of the dressing. Gently toss to combine. Add noodles and pour remaining dressing over top. Gently toss until evenly coated.

5. Transfer to a large bowl or platter. Add bean sprouts and half of the peanuts and toss gently. Sprinkle with green part of green onions, remaining 1 tbsp (15 mL) basil and peanuts. Top with cilantro, if using.

Variations

Add 1 cup (250 mL) steamed fresh vegetables, such as peas, soybeans, broccoli or corn, or sautéed shiitake mushrooms after the pepper is softened. You can also add 1 cup (250 mL) of any of the following or a combination thereof: bamboo shoots, water chestnuts and snow peas.

Full of flavor and nutrients, this tasty stew also makes a great side dish without the couscous.

Tip

Because can sizes vary, we provide a range of amounts for beans in our recipes. If using 19-oz (540 mL) cans, you may want to augment the spices with a pinch of cumin and curry powder to taste.

Couscous with Indian Vegetable Stew

½ cup	vanilla-flavor soy milk	125 mL
¼ cup	unsweetened shredded coconut	50 mL
2 tbsp	olive oil	25 mL
1	onion, finely chopped	1
3	cloves garlic, minced (about 1 tbsp/15 mL)	3
1	bulb fennel, stalks and core removed, cut into 1-inch (2.5 cm) thick strips	1
4 cups	chopped broccoli (florets and stems)	1 L
2	red bell peppers, cut into 1-inch (2.5 cm) pieces	2
1½ tbsp	ground cumin, divided	22 mL
1½ tbsp	finely grated gingerroot, or to taste	22 mL
1 tsp	curry powder	5 mL
½ tsp	ground cinnamon	2 mL
1	can (28 oz/796 mL) diced tomatoes, with juices	1
2	cans (each 14 to 19 oz/398 to 540 mL) chickpeas, drained and rinsed (see Tip, left), or 2 cups (500 mL) dried chickpeas, soaked, cooked and drained (see Legumes, page 13)	2
1 cup	vegetable stock	250 mL
1 tsp	granulated natural cane sugar, or to taste	5 mL
	Salt and freshly ground black pepper	
1 cup	couscous	250 mL

1. In a small saucepan over medium heat, combine soy milk with coconut. Cook over medium heat for 3 to 5 minutes or until mixture begins to simmer. Remove from heat and set aside.

2. In a large nonstick skillet or wok, heat oil over medium heat for 30 seconds. Add onion and cook, stirring, for 3 minutes or until softened. Add garlic and cook, stirring, for 1 minute. Stir in fennel, broccoli, red peppers, cumin, ginger, curry powder and cinnamon. Reduce heat to medium-low, cover and cook for 10 minutes or until vegetables are almost tender.

3. Stir in tomatoes, chickpeas and vegetable stock. Increase heat to medium-high and bring to a boil. Reduce heat to medium-low, cover and simmer for 10 minutes or until flavors blend. Add soy milk mixture, sugar and salt and pepper to taste, mixing well.

4. Meanwhile, prepare couscous according to package directions. Serve stew over couscous.

Risotto

The high starch content of Arborio rice, an Italian variety, contributes to the characteristic creamy texture of risotto. This tasty dish is comfort food for the whole family.

Tips

When making risotto, keep the rice submerged in liquid at all times. The frequent stirring helps develop the creamy texture, as does adding the liquid slowly and evenly.

In many locations, green onions are known as scallions.

3½ cups	vegetable stock	875 mL
3 tbsp	olive oil	45 mL
½ cup	chopped leek (white part only)	125 mL
½ cup	diced carrot	125 mL
1 cup	Arborio rice	250 mL
2	cloves garlic, minced (about 2 tsp/10 mL)	2
1	bay leaf	1
¾ cup	frozen peas, thawed and drained	175 mL
	Salt and freshly ground black pepper	
2	green onions (green and white parts), thinly sliced (see Tips, left)	2

1. In a pot, heat stock over low heat until simmering. Remove from heat.

2. In a heavy pot, heat oil over medium heat for 30 seconds. Add leeks and carrot and cook, stirring, for 4 minutes or until softened but not browned. Add rice and cook, stirring, for 2 minutes or until rice is coated with oil and heated through. Add garlic, bay leaf and 1 cup (250 mL) of the hot vegetable stock. Cook, stirring, for 30 seconds to prevent sticking. Add 1½ cups (375 mL) more stock, ½ cup (125 mL) at a time in three 4- to 5-minute intervals, stirring often, until the liquid is almost absorbed before adding more.

3. Stir in peas and ½ cup (125 mL) of the stock. Set the remaining ½ cup (125 mL) of the stock aside. Cook until rice is tender to the bite.

4. Stir in remaining stock just before serving to keep risotto soft and creamy. Remove bay leaf. Season with salt and freshly ground black pepper to taste. Top with green onions. Serve immediately.

Variations

For a richer result, stir in 2 tbsp (25 mL) soy margarine just before serving.

Substitute an equal amount of bell peppers, mushrooms and shallots for the carrots, peas and green onions, respectively.

Cheeseless Pizza *(page 113)*

Overleaf: Sticky Pecan Squares *(page 166)*

Corn Fritters

These fritters are a good way of using up fresh or frozen corn. They make a great breakfast served with maple syrup or fresh fruit. You can also serve them plain or topped with salsa, chutney or another condiment as an accompaniment to a main course.

Tip

If cutting fresh corn kernels from ears, scrape the cobs afterwards using the blunt side of a dinner knife to release remaining juices from the cob.

🍠 *Food processor or blender*

1 ½ cups	corn kernels, divided	375 mL
1 cup	plain soy milk	250 mL
6 tbsp	soft silken tofu (2 ½ oz/75 g)	90 mL
⅔ cup	yellow cornmeal	150 mL
6 tbsp	all-purpose flour	90 mL
2 tsp	granulated natural cane sugar or other dry sweetener	10 mL
½ tsp	salt	2 mL
¼ tsp	freshly ground black pepper	1 mL
3 tbsp	vegetable oil, divided	45 mL
Pinch	salt, optional	Pinch

1. In food processor or blender, combine ½ cup (125 mL) corn kernels with soy milk. Pulse eight to 10 times to release corn flavor into milk. Transfer to a bowl and add remaining corn kernels.

2. In another bowl, using a fork, mash tofu until smooth. Add cornmeal and continue mashing until a thick paste forms. Add to soy milk mixture, whisking until blended. Sprinkle with flour, sugar, salt and pepper. Using a wooden spoon, stir to make a smooth, thick batter.

3. In a skillet, heat 2 tbsp (25 mL) oil over high heat for 1 minute or until hot but not smoking. Working in batches, drop batter by spoonfuls (each about 2 tbsp/25 mL), 1 inch (2.5 cm) apart, into pan. Fry, turning once, for 2 to 3 minutes per side or until outside is browned and inside is firm. If the outside browns too quickly (in less than 2 minutes), reduce heat to medium. With a slotted spatula, transfer to a paper towel–lined plate to drain. Repeat with remaining batter, dividing and heating remaining 1 tbsp (15 mL) oil between batches as necessary. Sprinkle fritters with salt, if using, before serving.

Variations

Fold 1 tsp (5 mL) chopped fresh chives into the batter.

If you like Indian flavors, garnish with 1 tbsp (15 mL) coarsely chopped fresh cilantro leaves and accompany with mango chutney.

Pasta Puttanesca
(page 122)

Vegetable Fried Rice

This recipe can serve as either a side dish or a main course. While the rice is cooking, you can prepare the vegetables and sauce, making the entire preparation time less than 40 minutes.

Tips

Most supermarket chains carry canned straw mushrooms. If you can't find them, use 2 cups (500 mL) sliced mushrooms instead.

It is preferable to use a wok when making this dish, as the vegetables will cook faster and there will be more room to manipulate the ingredients.

Look for hot sesame oil in Asian markets or well-stocked supermarkets. If you can't find it, use regular or toasted sesame oil and a pinch of cayenne instead.

1 cup	jasmine, white or brown rice	250 mL
3 tbsp	peanut or vegetable oil, divided	45 mL
1	large onion, finely chopped (about 2 cups/500 mL)	1
3 cups	chopped bok choy	750 mL
1 cup	sugar snap peas, trimmed and cut into 1-inch (2.5 cm) pieces	250 mL
1	red bell pepper, thinly sliced and cut into 1-inch (2.5 cm) pieces	1
1	bunch green onions (white and green parts), coarsely chopped (about 1 cup/250 mL)	1
1	can (15 oz/450 mL) straw mushrooms (see Tips, left), drained	1
¼ cup	chopped fresh basil leaves	50 mL

SAUCE

½ cup	low-sodium soy sauce	125 mL
2 tbsp	distilled white vinegar	25 mL
1	clove garlic, minced (about 1 tsp/5 mL) or ¼ tsp (1 mL) garlic powder	1
1½ tsp	granulated natural cane sugar, or to taste	7 mL
	Hot sesame oil (see Tips, left)	

1. Cook rice according to package directions. Set aside.

2. In a large skillet or wok, heat 2 tbsp (25 mL) oil over medium heat for 30 seconds. Add onion and cook, stirring, for 3 minutes or until softened. Add bok choy, sugar snap peas, red pepper, green onions and mushrooms. Reduce heat to medium-low and cook, stirring occasionally, for 4 minutes or until vegetables are tender-crisp.

3. *Sauce:* Meanwhile, in a small bowl, whisk together soy sauce, vinegar, garlic, sugar and hot sesame oil to taste. Stir half into vegetables and add basil. Reduce heat to low, cover and cook for 10 minutes or until flavors are well blended. Transfer vegetables to a bowl and cover with foil to keep warm.

4. Return skillet to high heat and add remaining 1 tbsp (15 mL) oil. Heat until sizzling. Add rice and cook for 3 to 4 minutes, pushing down with a spatula to brown rice. Stir in vegetables and remaining sauce and mix well.

This slightly sweet rice is the perfect accompaniment to Curried Vegetables with Tofu (see recipe, page 98).

Tip

Depending on the type of stove you have and the kind of pot you are using, the cooking times may vary. Check rice after 30 minutes to see how much of the liquid has been absorbed. If there is liquid left, replace the lid and cook longer, lifting the lid as little as possible.

Coconut Rice

1	can (14 oz/398 mL) coconut milk	1
½ cup	vanilla-flavor soy milk	125 mL
1 cup	basmati or jasmine rice	250 mL
¼ tsp	salt, or to taste	1 mL
2 tbsp	unsweetened shredded coconut	25 mL

1. In a pot, bring coconut milk and soy milk just to a boil over medium–high heat. Watch carefully, because once the liquid reaches the boiling point, it will boil over.

2. Stir in rice and salt. Reduce heat to low, cover and cook for 30 to 40 minutes or until liquid is absorbed and rice is tender.

3. Fluff with a fork and stir in coconut. Serve immediately.

This dish is a favorite of Beth's stepdaughter, Valentine. It's comfort food at its best, topped with vibrant red pepper strips.

Tip

Roasted red peppers (they may be labeled sweet roasted red peppers or fire roasted red peppers) can be purchased in bottles and cans for much less than the price of fresh red bell peppers out of season, and they work well in this recipe. Substitute about 8 oz (250 g) roasted peppers for the fresh red peppers and reduce cooking time to 3 minutes.

Coconut-Flavored Polenta with Beans and Peppers

❧ *Preheat oven to 350°F (180°C)*

2 tbsp	vegetable oil	25 mL
1	small onion, finely diced	1
1	clove garlic, minced (about 1 tsp/5 mL)	1
¼ tsp	hot pepper flakes	1 mL
¼ tsp	ground allspice	1 mL
2	cans (each 14 oz/398 mL) coconut milk	2
1½ cups	cold water	375 mL
1 cup	medium-grain yellow cornmeal	250 mL
1½ tsp	salt	7 mL
1	can (14 to 19 oz/398 to 540 mL) red kidney beans, drained and rinsed, or 1 cup (250 mL) dried red kidney beans, soaked, cooked and drained (see Legumes, page 13)	1

TOPPING

2 tbsp	olive oil	25 mL
3	red bell peppers, cut in strips	3
	Salt and freshly ground black pepper	
¼ cup	water (approx)	50 mL

1. In an ovenproof pot, heat oil over medium heat for 30 seconds. Add onion and cook, stirring, for 3 minutes or until softened. Add garlic, hot pepper flakes and allspice and reduce heat to medium. Cook, stirring, for 1 minute to develop flavor. Stir in coconut milk.

2. In a bowl, whisk cold water with cornmeal. Add to pot, a little at a time, whisking vigorously to prevent lumps from forming. Gradually sprinkle in salt, whisking constantly.

3. Using a wooden spoon, stir polenta until the surface starts to bubble. Remove from heat and cover lightly with foil. Bake in preheated oven for 25 minutes, stirring after first 10 minutes, then every 5 minutes and stirring in beans at last interval, until polenta is very thick and beans are hot. Replace foil after each stir.

4. *Topping:* Meanwhile, in a large skillet, heat oil over medium-high heat for 30 seconds. Add red peppers and salt and pepper to taste and cook, stirring often, for 5 to 8 minutes or until soft, adding water as necessary to prevent scorching.

5. Spoon polenta into a large serving bowl and top with topping.

Lasagna with Spinach and Olives

➣ *Preheat oven to 375°F (190°C)*
➣ *13-by 9-inch (3 L) baking dish, greased*

1 lb	lasagna noodles (see Tips, left)	500 g
1/4 cup	all-purpose flour	50 mL
2 tbsp	olive oil	25 mL
3 cups	rice milk	750 mL
5	cloves garlic, minced (about 1 1/2 tbsp/22 mL)	5
1/2 tsp	dried rosemary leaves, crumbled	2 mL
1 1/2 lbs	silken tofu (extra-firm or firm), puréed	750 g
1/2 cup	oil-cured black olives, pitted and quartered	125 mL
	Salt and freshly ground black pepper	
2	packages (each 10 oz/300 g) frozen chopped spinach, thawed and drained (see Tips, left)	2
1	can (28 oz/796 mL) diced tomatoes, drained	1
2 cups	tomato sauce, divided (see Tips, left)	500 mL

1. Cook lasagna noodles according to package directions or use oven-ready noodles (see Tips, left).

2. In a pot over medium heat, combine flour with olive oil. Cook, stirring constantly, with a wooden spoon, for 30 seconds or until a thick paste forms (don't let it brown). Gradually add rice milk, whisking constantly to prevent lumps, until mixture thickens slightly, about 2 minutes. Stir in garlic and rosemary and cook for 30 seconds. Remove from heat and set aside.

3. In a bowl, combine puréed tofu, olives and ⅓ cup (75 mL) of the white sauce. Season with salt and pepper to taste.

4. In another bowl, combine spinach with ⅓ cup (75 mL) of the white sauce, making sure you get some of the rosemary and garlic, which may have settled at the bottom of the pot. Season with salt and pepper to taste.

5. In a third bowl, mix diced tomatoes with ½ cup (125 mL) tomato sauce.

6. Spread remaining tomato sauce over bottom of prepared baking dish. Cover with one-third of the lasagna noodles, overlapping or trimming as necessary to fit. Spread tofu mixture evenly over noodles. Cover with half of the remaining lasagna noodles. Spread spinach mixture evenly over noodles. Top with remaining lasagna noodles. Spread remaining white sauce over noodles evenly to moisten. Using a small spoon, dot the top of the dish with tomato mixture.

7. Cover with foil and bake for 35 to 40 minutes or until hot and bubbling. Let cool in dish for 5 to 10 minutes before serving. Using a metal spatula, cut into squares.

Variations

Substitute seasoned tomato sauce and diced tomatoes for the plain versions.

Replace rosemary with basil or oregano.

Tabbouleh

One of our all-time favorites, this salad, with its fresh and lively flavors of parsley and wheat spiked with mint, is very appealing.

Tips

This recipe can be doubled for a buffet or served as an hors d'oeuvres over Herbed Flatbread Chips (see recipe, page 37).

If you don't have a fresh tomato, substitute 1 tbsp (15 mL) chopped rehydrated sun-dried tomatoes.

In many locations, green onions are known as scallions.

¾ cup	medium or fine bulgur (cracked wheat)	175 mL
¾ cup	scalding hot water	175 mL
2	green onions (white and green parts), thinly sliced (see Tips, left)	2
3 tbsp	freshly squeezed lemon juice	45 mL
2 tbsp	olive oil	25 mL
1 tbsp	red wine vinegar	15 mL
1	bunch fresh Italian parsley, chopped (about 1 cup/250 mL)	1
2 tbsp	coarsely chopped fresh mint leaves (or 2 tsp/10 mL dried)	25 mL
1	plum tomato, coarsely chopped (see Tips, left)	1
¼ tsp	freshly ground black pepper	1 mL
¼ tsp	ground cumin	1 mL
½ tsp	salt, optional	2 mL

1. In a medium bowl, combine bulgur with hot water. Set aside for 10 minutes or until softened.

2. Add onions, lemon juice, olive oil and vinegar and stir well. Fold in parsley, mint, tomato, pepper, cumin and salt, if using.

3. Cover and refrigerate for at least 2 hours or until flavors are melded. Serve cold or let come to room temperature for maximum flavor.

> ## Variation
> Enhance this salad with chopped cucumbers, olives or bell peppers.

Penne with Mushroor...
Sun-Dried Tomatoes
and Artichokes

A little of this richly flavored sauce goes a long way. This is a great dish to serve to company. It's also a delicious way to use any leftover Baked Portobello Mushrooms (see recipe, page 152) and Roasted Bell Peppers (see recipe, page 151).

Tips

If you don't have homemade portobello mushrooms or roasted red peppers, look for marinated portobello mushrooms and roasted red peppers in jars or in the deli section of major supermarkets. Both work fine for this recipe.

If you want a more liquidy sauce, add ¼ cup (50 mL) tomato juice before adding the soy creamer.

3 tbsp	olive oil	45 mL
1	large sweet onion (such as Vidalia), thinly sliced	1
2	cloves garlic, minced (about 2 tsp/10 mL)	2
3	Baked Portobello Mushrooms (see recipe, page 152), thinly sliced	3
2	roasted red peppers (see Roasted Bell Peppers, page 151), peeled and thinly sliced	2
¾ cup	drained canned artichoke hearts, quartered	175 mL
¼ cup	coarsely chopped drained oil-packed sun-dried tomatoes	50 mL
8 oz	penne	250 g
½ cup	soy creamer	125 mL
1 tbsp	finely chopped fresh oregano leaves (or 1 tsp/5 mL dried)	15 mL
	Salt and freshly ground black pepper	

1. In a large nonstick skillet, heat oil over medium–low heat for 30 seconds. Add onion and cook for 12 minutes or until very soft and lightly browned.

2. Add garlic and cook, stirring, for 1 minute. Add portobello mushrooms, roasted red peppers, artichoke hearts and sun-dried tomatoes and cook, stirring, for 5 to 7 minutes or until vegetables are tender.

3. Meanwhile, in a large pot of boiling salted water, cook penne for 8 minutes or according to package instructions, until tender to the bite.

4. Add soy creamer and oregano to vegetable mixture and stir well. Cook for 5 minutes longer to blend flavors. Divide hot penne among serving bowls and spoon vegetable mixture over top and season with salt and pepper to taste.

This richly flavored dish is surprisingly simple to make. It's a great meal to serve to company, accompanied by a fresh, vibrant salad and crusty bread.

Tip

Soy creamer is used in the same way that traditional cream is. It is rich and creamy but lower in saturated fat than its dairy counterpart.

Rotini with Mushrooms and Caramelized Onions

3 tbsp	olive oil	45 mL
1	large onion, thinly sliced	1
2	cloves garlic, minced (about 2 tsp/10 mL), divided	2
8 oz	button mushrooms, thinly sliced (about 2 cups/500 mL)	250 g
6 oz	oyster mushrooms, halved (about ¾ cup/175 mL)	175 g
2	Baked Portobello Mushrooms (see recipe, page 152), halved and thinly sliced	2
8 oz	rotini	250 g
⅓ cup	sweet Marsala wine, divided	75 mL
2 tbsp	soy creamer (see Tip, left)	25 mL
	Salt and freshly ground black pepper	

1. In a large skillet, heat 2 tbsp (25 mL) olive oil over medium-high heat until very hot but not smoking. Add onion and drizzle with remaining olive oil. Reduce heat to low, cover and cook, stirring every 10 minutes to prevent burning and sticking, for 25 to 30 minutes or until onions are soft and brown.

2. Add half of the garlic and cook, stirring, for 1 minute. Increase heat to medium–low and add button, oyster and portobello mushrooms. Stir well, cover and cook for 5 to 6 minutes or until mushrooms begin to soften.

3. Meanwhile, in a large pot of boiling salted water, cook rotini for 8 minutes or according to package instructions, until tender to the bite. Drain.

4. Add ¼ cup (50 mL) Marsala to mushroom mixture and cook, uncovered, for 4 minutes. Add soy creamer and mix well. Reduce heat to low and cook for 1 minute. Add rotini and toss gently to coat. Stir in remaining Marsala, garlic, and salt and pepper to taste. Cook, stirring constantly, for 1 minute or until flavors are blended.

Variation

Any blend of fresh mushrooms works well in this recipe. You can replace button or oyster mushrooms with cremini, shiitake or chanterelle, using the same amounts as those that you are replacing.

Bow Tie Pasta Salad

This vibrant salad adds color and zest to any meal. It's a welcome addition to a potluck dinner and makes a nice side dish or snack. It's convenient, too, as you can keep the leftovers in your refrigerator for 3 or 4 days.

Tips

If you are using large (fat) carrots, cut them in half lengthwise before slicing.

The amount of salt you need to add will vary depending on the olives you use. If you are using kalamata or oil-cured olives, you will need less salt than if you are using canned olives.

8 oz	bow tie (farfalle) or other short pasta	250 g
1 cup	broccoli florets	250 mL
1 cup	coarsely chopped cauliflower	250 mL
1 cup	thinly sliced carrots (see Tips, left)	250 mL
1	small zucchini, halved lengthwise and cut into 1/4-inch (1 cm) thick slices	1
1 cup	pitted kalamata olives, halved	250 mL
Half	red onion, halved and very thinly sliced (about 1 cup/250 mL)	Half

VINAIGRETTE

1 cup	red wine vinegar	250 mL
1/3 cup	olive oil	75 mL
1 1/2 tbsp	granulated natural cane sugar or other dry sweetener	22 mL
2	cloves garlic, minced (about 2 tsp/10 mL)	2
1/2 tsp	Dijon mustard	2 mL
1/2 tsp	dried tarragon leaves	2 mL
1/4 tsp	freshly ground black pepper, or to taste	1 mL
	Salt	

1. In a large pot of boiling salted water, cook pasta for 8 minutes or according to package instructions, until tender to the bite. Drain.

2. *Vinaigrette:* In a large bowl, whisk together vinegar, olive oil, sugar, garlic, mustard, tarragon, pepper and salt to taste.

3. Add broccoli, cauliflower, carrots, zucchini, olives and onion to vinaigrette. Mix well.

4. Add hot pasta and mix well. Cover and refrigerate for at least 3 hours or until flavors are blended, or for up to 4 days.

Strictly Vegetables

Ratatouille

Tips

If you don't like the bitter flavor of some eggplant, salting it with coarse salt, such as kosher or sea salt, and allowing it to "sweat" reduces some of the bitterness.

Use canned tomatoes with or without seasoning for this recipe.

Ratatouille will keep, covered, in the refrigerator for up to 3 days.

1	eggplant (about 1 1/4 lb/625 g), unpeeled (see Tips, left) and cut into 1/2-inch (1 cm) cubes	1
2 tbsp	kosher or coarse sea salt	25 mL
3 tbsp	olive or vegetable oil	45 mL
1	large onion, sliced on the vertical (1/4 inch/0.5 cm)	1
5	cloves garlic, minced (about 1 1/2 tbsp/22 mL)	5
2	green bell peppers, cut into 1/2-inch (1 cm) squares	2
2	zucchini, quartered lengthwise and cut into 1/2-inch (1 cm) thick slices	2
1/3 cup	dry white wine, water or vegetable stock	75 mL
1	bay leaf	1
1 tsp	dried thyme leaves	5 mL
1	can (28 oz/796 mL) diced tomatoes, with juices (see Tips, left)	1
	Salt and freshly ground black pepper	
2 tbsp	chopped fresh Italian parsley	25 mL

1. In a colander over the sink, toss eggplant with salt. Let drain for 20 minutes. Rinse and pat dry.

2. In a large pot, heat oil over medium heat for 30 seconds. Add onion and cook, stirring, for 3 minutes or until softened. Add garlic and cook, stirring, for 1 minute. Add eggplant and cook, stirring occasionally, for 5 minutes. Add peppers and cook, stirring, for 1 minute.

3. Stir in zucchini, white wine, bay leaf, thyme and tomatoes and cook until small bubbles begin to form on surface. Reduce heat to maintain a gentle simmer. Cover and cook, stirring occasionally, for 15 to 20 minutes or until eggplant is tender and mixture is thickened. Season with salt and pepper to taste. Discard bay leaf. Serve hot, let cool to room temperature or cover, chill and serve cold. Sprinkle with parsley before serving.

Variation

Use red, yellow or orange bell peppers instead of the green peppers. Add 1 cup (250 mL) quartered button mushrooms along with the peppers.

Eggplant with Garlicky Hoisin Sauce

Not only is eggplant a very versatile vegetable but it is also high in fiber and available year-round, which makes it a staple in the vegan diet. Serve this dish over your favorite type of steamed rice.

Tips

Whole eggplant can be stored for 3 or 4 days in a cool, dry place. When purchasing eggplant, look for smooth, firm skin.

In many locations, green onions are known as scallions.

1	large eggplant (about 1 ½ lbs/750 g), halved lengthwise then crosswise and cut lengthwise into ⅛-inch (0.25 cm) thick strips	1
2 tbsp	kosher or coarse sea salt	25 mL
2 tbsp	sesame oil	25 mL
2	cloves garlic, minced (about 2 tsp/10 mL)	2
2	red bell peppers, cut lengthwise into 1-inch (2.5 cm) strips	2
1 cup	coarsely chopped green onions (white and light green parts), see Tips, left	250 mL
1 cup	mushrooms, thinly sliced	250 mL

SAUCE

3	cloves garlic, minced (about 1 tbsp/15 mL)	3
⅓ cup	hoisin sauce	75 mL
1 tbsp	low-sodium soy sauce	15 mL
2 tsp	seasoned rice vinegar	10 mL
½ tsp	sesame oil	2 mL
½ tsp	hot sesame oil, or to taste	2 mL
	Granulated natural cane sugar	

1. In a colander over the sink, toss eggplant with salt. Let drain for 20 minutes. Rinse and pat dry.

2. *Sauce:* In a small bowl, whisk together garlic, hoisin sauce, soy sauce, rice vinegar, sesame oil and hot sesame oil. Add sugar to taste. Set aside.

3. In a large nonstick skillet or wok, heat sesame oil over medium–high heat for 30 seconds. Add garlic and cook, stirring, for 30 seconds. Add eggplant and red peppers and cook, stirring often, for 5 minutes. Stir in green onions and mushrooms. Add half of the sauce and reduce heat to low. Cover and simmer for 10 minutes or until vegetables are tender. Add reserved sauce and cook for 3 minutes or until flavors are developed.

Veggie Kabobs

Tips

Zucchini, which comes in green and yellow (or golden) versions, is a type of summer squash. In this recipe we like to use both green zucchini and yellow summer squash for appearance. If you prefer, use just green or golden zucchini in this recipe.

The longer the marinating time, the deeper the flavors.

Any leftover veggies from these kabobs make a perfect beginning for tasty pasta dishes or salads.

❧ Preheat grill or broiler
❧ 16 bamboo or metal skewers

⅓ cup	freshly squeezed lemon juice	75 mL
¼ cup	olive oil	50 mL
1	clove garlic, minced (about 1 tsp/5 mL)	1
2 tsp	dried oregano leaves (or 2 tbsp/25 mL finely chopped fresh)	10 mL
	Salt and freshly ground black pepper	
2	bell peppers (any color), cut into 1-inch (2.5 cm) strips	2
2	small zucchini, cut into 1-inch (2.5 cm) thick slices	2
2 cups	grape tomatoes or cherry tomatoes (about 16)	500 mL
2 cups	whole button mushrooms (about 16)	500 mL
1	large onion, cut into 8 wedges and halved crosswise, separated into single layers	1
1	yellow summer squash (such as golden zucchini) cut into 1-inch (2.5 cm) cubes	1

1. In a large bowl or resealable plastic bag, combine lemon juice, olive oil, garlic, oregano and salt and pepper to taste. Add peppers, zucchini, tomatoes, mushrooms, onion and squash and stir to evenly coat. Marinate at room temperature for 15 to 20 minutes or in the refrigerator for up to 12 hours.

2. Thread vegetables onto skewers, alternating to form an attractive pattern and leaving a bit of space between the pieces to allow air to circulate.

3. Grill or broil, turning and basting often with remaining marinade, for 8 to 10 minutes or until vegetables are browned on all sides and tender. While cooking, rotate location of the skewers on the grill or broiler to ensure even cooking.

Variations

Vary the flavor by replacing oregano with the same quantity of thyme, basil or rosemary.

Substitute garlic salt for the fresh garlic, but adjust seasoning accordingly.

The vegetables (unskewered) can also be spread in a single layer on two greased rimmed baking sheets and baked in a preheated 400°F (200°C) oven for 30 to 35 minutes. Turn the vegetables and rotate the pans after 20 minutes.

For convenience, cook the vegetables in a nonstick grill basket, being aware that some may cook more quickly than others.

Broccoli and Red Peppers with Lime-Ginger Soy Sauce

This a great side dish but it makes a satisfying main course, served over rice or couscous with added vegetables or tofu (see Variations, below).

Tips

If you prefer broccoli bright green and crisp, cook it for about 8 minutes. Ten minutes will produce a more tender result.

In many locations, green onions are known as scallions.

1 tbsp	sesame oil	15 mL
2	cloves garlic, minced (about 2 tsp/10 mL)	2
2	large red bell peppers, cut lengthwise into ¼-inch (0.5 cm) thick strips	2
5 cups	chopped broccoli (florets and stems)	1.25 L
¼ cup	finely chopped green onions (white and light green parts), see Tips, left	50 mL
1 tsp	toasted sesame seeds	5 mL

SAUCE

2	cloves garlic, minced	2
¼ cup	seasoned rice vinegar	50 mL
2 tbsp	low-sodium soy sauce	25 mL
1½ tbsp	freshly squeezed lime juice	22 mL
2 tsp	grated gingerroot	10 mL
½ tsp	granulated natural cane sugar, optional	2 mL
Dash	hot sesame oil, or to taste	Dash

1. *Sauce:* In a bowl, whisk together garlic, rice vinegar, soy sauce, lime juice, ginger, sugar, if using, and hot sesame oil.

2. In a large nonstick skillet or wok, heat sesame oil over medium heat for 30 seconds. Add garlic and cook, stirring, for 1 minute or until fragrant but not browned. Stir in peppers, broccoli and green onions. Reduce heat to low. Cover and cook, stirring occasionally, for 8 to 10 minutes or until broccoli is tender but not limp. Add sauce and stir well. Reduce heat to low and cook for 2 minutes or until hot. Transfer to a serving bowl and sprinkle with sesame seeds.

Variations

To serve this as a main course, add more vegetables along with the broccoli. We like the combination of 1 cup (250 mL) baby corn; 1 cup (250 mL) canned straw mushrooms, drained; and 1 can (5 oz/150 g) bamboo shoots. If you prefer, add cubes of Asian-Style Baked Tofu (see recipe, page 101) in the amount that suits your tastes.

Replace sesame seeds with 1 tbsp (15 mL) toasted pine nuts.

*The texture of mashed
potatoes is really a matter of
taste. Some like them smooth,
others prefer the odd lump
or two. Whichever you prefer,
these flavorful potatoes are
a great accompaniment to
many dishes.*

Tip

If you prefer a creamy
texture and don't have
a ricer, try using an
immersion blender. Be
sure not to overblend
the potatoes because they
can easily become gluey.
To ensure that you don't
overprocess, move the
wand around to different
parts of the pot.

Garlic Mashed Potatoes

4	large potatoes, peeled and cut in half	4
3 tbsp	soy margarine	45 mL
4	cloves garlic, minced (about 4 tsp/20 mL)	4
1 cup	vanilla-flavor or plain soy milk	250 mL
	Salt and freshly ground black pepper	

1. In a large pot, combine potatoes with cold water to cover, then bring to a boil over high heat. Reduce heat to low and simmer for 25 to 30 minutes or until potatoes are easily pierced with a fork. Drain and return to pot.

2. Meanwhile, in a small saucepan, melt margarine over low heat until bubbling. Add garlic and cook, stirring, for 30 to 60 seconds or until fragrant but not browned. Add soy milk. Increase heat to medium and bring to a boil. Remove from heat and let steep while mashing potatoes.

3. Using a potato masher, mash potatoes. (If you prefer a smoother texture, put the potatoes through a ricer.) Add soy milk mixture, stirring constantly until desired consistency is achieved. Season with salt and pepper to taste. Mix well.

Variation

Add 2 tbsp (25 mL) finely chopped fresh chives or garlic chives along with the soy milk. Serve with vegan sour cream alternative on the side.

Serve these tasty hash browns for breakfast with soy bacon and whole wheat toast, or as a side dish to accompany veggie burgers or hot dogs.

Tip

The potatoes may break up a bit in the process of frying. That's fine. They are best when crumbly and browned.

Spicy Hash Brown Potatoes

4	large baking potatoes (unpeeled)	4
2 tbsp	vegetable oil	25 mL
2	small onions, finely chopped	2
3	cloves garlic, minced (about 1 tbsp/15 mL)	3
1/4 tsp	cayenne pepper, or to taste	1 mL
	Salt and freshly ground black pepper	

1. In a large pot, combine potatoes with cold water to cover, then bring to a boil over high heat. Reduce heat to low and simmer for 15 to 18 minutes or until potatoes are easily pierced with a fork. Drain and rinse under cold water. When the potatoes are cool enough to handle, cut into 1/2-inch (1 cm) cubes.

2. In a large nonstick skillet, heat oil over high heat for 1 minute or until hot but not smoking. Add onions and garlic and cook, stirring, for 3 minutes or until onions are softened. Add potatoes and mix well. Stir in cayenne pepper, and salt and pepper to taste. Press down on the potatoes with a spatula for 3 minutes or until browned, then flip over and cook for 2 to 3 minutes or until browned and crisp.

Variations

Add 1 tbsp (15 mL) of your favorite chopped fresh herb to pan along with the potatoes.

For a less spicy but equally flavorful result, substitute ancho chili powder for the cayenne pepper.

This is one of our favorite ways of cooking asparagus, because it captures its intense flavor. This dish is equally enjoyable hot and at room temperature.

Tips

To trim asparagus, snap off the bottom of the stalk, where it is woody and fibrous.

Be sure to keep the lid on the pot during cooking to maintain a high cooking temperature. The cooking time will vary depending upon the thickness of the asparagus. Test with the tines of a fork: if the stalk can be pierced easily, it is done.

Asparagus with Capers

Dutch oven with tight-fitting lid, 12 inches (30 cm) in diameter or larger

1 lb	asparagus, trimmed	500 g
3 tbsp	olive oil, divided	45 mL
¼ tsp	salt	1 mL
2 tbsp	white wine vinegar	25 mL
1 tbsp	capers, with brine	15 mL
1	slice toast or stale dry bread, torn into ½-inch (1 cm) pieces	1
2 tbsp	coarsely chopped fresh Italian parsley	25 mL
	Freshly ground black pepper	

1. Rinse asparagus and leave wet. In Dutch oven, heat 2 tbsp (25 mL) olive oil over high heat for 1 minute or until hot but not smoking. Add wet asparagus and sprinkle with salt. Immediately cover pot. Using thick pot holders to hold the lid in place, cook constantly and vigorously jiggling the pot (as you would when making popcorn) for 4 to 6 minutes or until asparagus is tender. Transfer to a serving dish.

2. Reduce heat to medium. To same pot, add remaining oil, vinegar and capers with brine and mix well. Stir in bread and parsley and immediately spoon over asparagus. Season with pepper to taste.

Variation

Substitute toasted pine nuts for the bread or use them as an enhancement sprinkled over the finished dish. To toast, place 2 tbsp (25 mL) pine nuts in a small dry skillet over medium heat. Cook, stirring constantly, for 3 to 4 minutes or until they are evenly toasted.

Tangy Green Beans

A robust citrus vinaigrette combined with subtle-tasting green beans makes for a great combination of flavors.

1 tbsp	sesame oil	15 mL
3 cups	chopped trimmed green beans (1-inch/2.5 cm pieces)	750 mL

CITRUS VINAIGRETTE

1 tbsp	grated orange zest	15 mL
1/3 cup	freshly squeezed orange juice	75 mL
1/3 cup	rice vinegar	75 mL
1/4 cup	vegetable oil	50 mL
1/4 tsp	Dijon mustard	1 mL
2	cloves garlic, minced (about 2 tsp/10 mL)	2
1/4 tsp	grated gingerroot	1 mL

1. *Vinaigrette:* In a serving bowl, whisk together orange zest and juice, rice vinegar, oil, mustard, garlic and ginger. Set aside.

2. In a nonstick skillet, heat sesame oil over medium heat for 1 minute. Add green beans, reduce heat to low and cook, stirring, for 3 to 4 minutes or until coated and bright green. Add to vinaigrette and toss well. Let stand for 5 minutes or until flavors are blended. Serve immediately.

Variations

To add taste and texture, sprinkle with slivered almonds just before serving.

If you're trying to reduce your dietary fat intake, steam the beans for 3 to 4 minutes instead of frying them and omit the sesame oil. Toss with vinaigrette as directed.

Roasted Bell Peppers

These multipurpose peppers are always great to have on hand, as they can be used in a number of recipes. Use a variety of colored peppers, such as yellow, red, orange and green, to add vibrancy to pasta sauces and salads or to use in one of the variations below.

Tip

If some of the skin adheres to the flesh after the peppers have cooled, use your fingers to peel it off. Marinating peppers in balsamic vinegar extends their shelf life (see Variations, below).

❧ *Preheat oven to 350°F (180°C)*
❧ *13-by-9 inch (3 L) baking dish, greased*

3	bell peppers, seeds and ribs removed and quartered	3
2 tbsp	garlic-infused oil	25 mL
1 tbsp	garlic powder	15 mL
	Salt and freshly ground black pepper	

1. Place peppers in prepared baking dish. Brush both sides of each pepper piece with garlic oil and sprinkle with garlic powder and salt and pepper to taste. Bake for 45 to 50 minutes or until very soft and wrinkled.

2. Transfer to a bowl, cover with a plate and let cool to room temperature. The skins will naturally separate from the flesh of the pepper (see Tip, left). Store in an airtight container and refrigerate for up to 4 days.

Variations

Balsamic Marinated Peppers: Cut peeled roasted peppers into quarters. Add ½ cup (125 mL) balsamic vinegar and toss to coat. Cover and refrigerate for 8 hours or for up to 1 week.

Garlic Marinated Peppers: Toss peeled roasted peppers with 2 cloves garlic, thinly sliced, and ¼ cup (50 mL) extra-virgin olive oil. Marinate for several hours or overnight, then remove the garlic. Add sea salt and freshly ground black pepper to taste and serve immediately.

Baked Portobello Mushrooms

Baked portobello mushrooms have many uses in the vegan kitchen. They can be sliced and added to salads and sauces or served whole on a bun for a satisfying sandwich.

Tip

When removing the mushroom stem, carefully cut it out with a paring knife to leave the mushroom cap intact.

🌿 *Preheat oven to 350°F (180°C)*
🌿 *13-by 9-inch (3 L) baking dish, greased*

| 4 | portobello mushrooms, cleaned and stems removed (see Tips, left) | 4 |

MARINADE

¼ cup	olive oil	50 mL
2 tbsp	balsamic vinegar	25 mL
	Salt and freshly ground pepper	

1. *Marinade:* In a small bowl, whisk together olive oil, balsamic vinegar and salt and pepper to taste.

2. Place mushrooms in prepared baking dish, gill side up, and pour marinade over top, making sure each mushroom cap is completely covered. Cover dish and refrigerate for 1 to 2 hours to allow mushrooms to absorb some of the marinade.

3. Drain off excess marinade. Bake mushrooms in preheated oven for 35 minutes or until soft.

Variations

Portobello Mushroom Burgers: Serve whole baked mushrooms on a bun or soft roll.

Portobello Mushroom Burgers with Caramelized Onions: For a nice change, top burgers with caramelized onions. To caramelize onions, melt 2 tbsp (25 mL) soy margarine in a skillet over medium heat. Add 1 large onion, thinly sliced. Sprinkle with 1 tsp (5 mL) granulated natural cane sugar and cook, stirring often, for 20 minutes or until onion is soft and lightly browned.

Curried Zucchini Strips

Tip

Leftovers of this dish are
delicious. Eat them on
their own or cut them into
chunks and add to a salad
or stir-fry.

3	zucchini	3
1 tbsp	vegetable oil	15 mL
¼ tsp	curry powder	1 mL
	Salt	

1. Cut ends off zucchini. Cut in half lengthwise, then cut each half in half crosswise. Cut each quarter lengthwise into two or three strips of equal size. These will vary depending on the size of your zucchini.

2. In a large nonstick skillet, heat oil over medium-high heat until hot but not smoking. Add zucchini and cook, stirring occasionally for 5 minutes or until soft.

3. Sprinkle with curry powder and salt to taste, and mix well. Cover and cook for 2 minutes or until tender and fragrant.

Tomato Sauce

This sauce has many uses. Serve it over pasta, as the base for lasagna or with other Italian-style dishes.

Tip

Canned tomatoes, diced or whole, often come with added flavors, such as roasted garlic and basil, roasted red peppers or Italian seasoning. All work well in this sauce.

⋟Blender, food processor or immersion blender

2 tbsp	olive oil	25 mL
1	large onion, finely diced	1
3	cloves garlic, minced (about 1 tbsp/15 mL)	3
1½ cups	mushrooms, finely chopped	375 mL
2	cans (each 28 oz/796 mL) diced tomatoes, with juices	2
1 tbsp	tomato paste	15 mL
1	bay leaf	1
1 tbsp	dried basil leaves (or 3 tbsp/45 mL finely chopped fresh)	15 mL
1 tbsp	dried oregano leaves (or 3 tbsp/45 mL finely chopped fresh)	15 mL
1 tsp	garlic powder	5 mL
¼ tsp	freshly ground black pepper, or to taste	1 mL
2 tbsp	red wine vinegar	25 mL
2 tsp	granulated natural cane sugar, or to taste	10 mL
	Salt	

1. In a pot, heat oil over medium heat for 30 seconds. Add onion and cook, stirring, for 3 minutes or until softened. Add garlic and cook, stirring, for 1 minute. Add mushrooms and cook, stirring, for 3 minutes or until soft.

2. Add tomatoes, tomato paste, bay leaf, basil, oregano, garlic powder and pepper and bring to a boil. Reduce heat to low. Stir in vinegar, sugar and salt to taste. Simmer, uncovered, stirring occasionally, for 15 minutes. Remove from heat and let cool for 10 minutes.

3. In blender or food processor, working in 2 or 3 batches (or using an immersion blender in the pot), purée sauce until smooth. If necessary, return to pot. Reheat over medium heat until bubbling.

Variation

Add ingredients such as finely chopped bell peppers or pitted black olives to this sauce. Add vegetables that need to be softened, such as bell peppers, celery or carrots, along with the onion. If you like a bit of heat, add a pinch of hot pepper flakes along with the garlic powder.

Sweet potatoes, which are loaded with beta-carotene, are delicious when made into a crispy cake. Beth's family likes them as an accompaniment to a main course of black beans, with green salad and whole-grain bread.

Tips

One large or two small sweet potatoes weigh about 1 lb (500 g).

If you prefer, substitute 1 tsp (5 mL) dried basil and/or parsley for the fresh.

For added crispness, place cakes in 375°F (190°C) oven for 10 minutes after they are finished cooking.

Crispy Sweet Potato Cakes

1 lb	sweet potato, peeled and grated	500 g
1 tbsp	finely chopped fresh basil leaves	15 mL
1 tbsp	chopped fresh Italian parsley	15 mL
1 tbsp	orange juice	15 mL
½ tsp	salt	2 mL
¼ tsp	freshly ground black pepper	1 mL
3 tbsp	all-purpose flour, divided	45 mL
	Vegetable oil for frying	
	Salt, optional	

1. In a bowl, combine sweet potato, basil, parsley, orange juice, salt and pepper. Set aside for 15 minutes to draw out juices. Sprinkle 1 tbsp (15 mL) flour over top and stir well. Divide mixture into 12 equal portions.

2. Lightly dust work surface with 1 tbsp (15 mL) of the remaining flour. Place portions of sweet potato mixture on the work surface. Using hands, roll each into a ball. Sprinkle with remaining flour, evenly covering the outside of each ball.

3. Into a large skillet, pour oil to a depth of a ¼ inch (0.5 cm). Heat over high heat for 30 seconds or until hot but not smoking. Working in batches as necessary, place balls in skillet, about 2 inches (5 cm) apart. Using a metal spatula, press each flat into a patty shape. Reduce heat to medium-high and cook, turning and checking bottoms to ensure even cooking, for 2 to 3 minutes per side or until well browned and crispy. Transfer to a paper towel–lined plate and keep warm. Repeat with remaining cakes, adding and heating oil as necessary between batches.

4. Sprinkle with salt, if using, before serving. Serve immediately or let cool, cover and refrigerate for up to 3 days. Reheat in 375°F (190°C) oven for 10 minutes.

Variations

Make these cakes using equal amounts of sweet potato and another vegetable. Mix 8 oz (250 g) white potatoes, carrots, parsnips or turnips, peeled and grated, with 8 oz (250 g) sweet potato.

If you like the taste of orange, add ½ tsp (2 mL) grated orange zest to the mixture.

Cubed Sweet Potato Fries

These potatoes go well with almost any main dish. They hold up well in a warm oven, so they can be prepared in advance for guests. Their small cubed shape makes them convenient for a buffet, too.

↬ *Preheat oven to 375°F (190°C)*
↬ *Large rimmed baking sheet, greased*

1 tbsp	packed brown sugar or other dry sweetener	15 mL
½ tsp	ground ginger	2 mL
½ tsp	curry powder	2 mL
½ tsp	salt	2 mL
¼ tsp	ground allspice	1 mL
¼ tsp	ground cardamom, optional	1 mL
⅛ tsp	cayenne pepper	0.5 mL
3	sweet potatoes (about 8 oz/250 g each), peeled and cut into 1-inch (2.5 cm) cubes	3
3 tbsp	olive oil	45 mL
1	lemon, halved, divided	1

1. In a small bowl, combine sugar, ginger, curry powder, salt, allspice, cardamom, if using, and cayenne pepper.

2. In a bowl, toss potato cubes with oil until evenly coated. Squeeze the juice of one lemon half over the mixture and toss well. Sprinkle with spice mixture and stir to coat evenly.

3. Spread potatoes in a single layer on prepared baking sheet. Bake, turning cubes twice, for 40 to 45 minutes or until evenly browned outside and tender inside. Squeeze juice of remaining lemon half over potatoes and toss gently before serving.

Variation

Serve these potatoes at a Mexican brunch and customize the spice mix to suit the theme. Use ½ tsp (2 mL) ground cumin, ½ tsp (2 mL) garlic powder, ½ tsp (2 mL) chili powder, ½ tsp (2 mL) salt, ¼ tsp (1 mL) ground cinnamon and ¼ tsp (1 mL) freshly ground black pepper. Substitute a lime for the lemon.

Roasted Vegetables in Phyllo Cups

Improvise when serving this dish by using seasonal vegetables and varying the herbs and seasonings. It is a wonderful party dish. Guests are impressed with the delicate ruffled edges of the phyllo cups.

Tips

If you don't like the bitter flavor of some eggplant, salting it with coarse salt, such as sea salt or kosher salt, and allowing it to "sweat" reduces some of the bitterness.

Save any leftover roasted vegetables for use in pasta dishes or stir-fries.

❧ *Preheat oven to 375°F (190°C)*
❧ *Large rimmed baking sheet, greased*

1	small eggplant, peeled and cut into $1/2$-inch (1 cm) cubes (see Tips, left)	1
2 tbsp	kosher or coarse sea salt	25 mL
1	red bell pepper, cut into $1/2$-inch (1 cm) cubes	1
1	summer squash or golden zucchini, cut into $1/2$-inch (1 cm) cubes	1
1	medium sweet potato, peeled and cut into $1/2$-inch (1 cm) cubes	1
1	small red onion, cut into $1/2$-inch (1 cm) cubes	1
$1/4$ cup	freshly squeezed lemon juice, divided	50 mL
$1/4$ cup	olive oil	50 mL
1 tbsp	dried oregano leaves	15 mL
$1/2$ tsp	salt, or to taste	2 mL
$1/4$ tsp	freshly ground black pepper	1 mL
12	Phyllo Cups (see recipe, page 173)	12

1. In a colander over the sink, toss eggplant with salt. Let drain for 20 minutes. Rinse and pat dry.

2. In a large bowl, combine eggplant, red pepper, squash, sweet potato and onion. Sprinkle with 2 tbsp (25 mL) lemon juice, olive oil, oregano, salt and pepper and toss to mix thoroughly.

3. Spread in a single layer on prepared baking sheet. Roast in preheated oven, turning vegetables and rotating pans halfway through, for 40 minutes or until vegetables are tender, browned and fragrant. Sprinkle remaining 2 tbsp (25 mL) lemon juice over vegetables and toss well.

4. Fill each phyllo cup with a heaping spoonful of vegetables. Serve hot or at room temperature.

these tasty potatoes
*with any main course or use
them to make Roasted Red
Potato Salad (see recipe,
page 64).*

Tip

When cutting potatoes for
this recipe, make sure most
chunks contain some skin.

Roasted Red Potatoes

🌿 *Preheat oven to 450°F (230°C)*
🌿 *13-by 9-inch (3 L) baking dish*

3 lbs	red potatoes (unpeeled), cut into ¼- to ½-inch (0.5 cm to 1 cm) cubes	1.5 kg
¼ cup	olive oil	50 mL
2 tsp	garlic powder	10 mL
½ tsp	salt, or to taste	2 mL
½ tsp	freshly ground black pepper	2 mL

1. In a large bowl, combine potatoes, oil, garlic powder, salt and pepper. Toss until evenly coated. Transfer to baking dish.
2. Bake, rotating dish halfway through, for 40 minutes or until potatoes are browned and crispy outside and tender inside. Serve immediately.

> ## Variation
> Instead of using garlic powder, mix 2 cloves garlic, minced, with the olive oil, salt and pepper. Add potatoes and toss until evenly coated.

Desserts and Baked Goods

Almond Cookies

Tips

You can also mix this
dough by hand. In a
mixing bowl, combine
flour and sugar. Using
two knives, a pastry
blender or your fingers,
cut in margarine until
mixture resembles coarse
crumbs. Add almond
extract and mix with
a fork until blended.
Continue with recipe.

These cookies are even
better the day after you
bake them. Store them in
an airtight container for
up to 4 days or freeze
them in a resealable plastic
bag for up to 2 months.

➣ *Preheat oven to 300°F (150°C)*
➣ *Food processor*
➣ *Rimless cookie sheet, ungreased*

2 cups	all-purpose flour	500 mL
1 cup	cold soy margarine	250 mL
1 cup	granulated natural cane sugar	250 mL
1 tsp	almond extract	5 mL
¼ cup	slivered almonds (approx)	50 mL

1. In food processor fitted with metal blade, combine flour, margarine, sugar and almond extract. Process for 20 seconds or until crumbly (see Tips, left).

2. Shape the dough into 1-inch (2.5 cm) balls. Place on baking sheet, about 1½ inches (4 cm) apart. Press down lightly with a spoon to flatten. (Cookies will be approximately 1½ inches/4 cm in diameter.) Press three slivered almonds into the top of each cookie.

3. Bake in preheated oven for 25 minutes or until light brown around the edges. Let cool on pan on a rack for 15 minutes, then transfer to rack and let cool completely.

Variation

If you prefer a cookie that is less sweet, reduce sugar to
⅔ cup (150 mL).

Veggie Kabobs (page 144)

These easy-to-make favorites go fast in our households and are tastier than their traditional counterpart.

Tip

Commercial peanut butter works very well in this recipe. If you're using salted peanut butter, reduce the salt to ¼ tsp (1 mL).

Peanut Butter Cookies

❧ *Preheat oven to 350°F (180°C)*
❧ *Rimless cookie sheets, ungreased*

¾ cup	all-purpose flour	175 mL
1 tsp	baking soda	5 mL
1 tsp	salt	5 mL
1 cup	smooth natural peanut butter, stirred well before measuring (see Tip, left)	250 mL
1 cup	packed light brown sugar or granulated natural cane sugar	250 mL
3 tbsp	puréed silken tofu	45 mL
1 tsp	vanilla	5 mL
1 tsp	water	5 mL

1. In a small bowl, combine flour, baking soda and salt.

2. In a separate bowl, mix peanut butter with sugar until well blended. Stir in tofu, vanilla and water. Add flour mixture and mix until well blended. Using floured hands, knead mixture for about 1 minute to form smooth dough.

3. Shape dough into 1-inch (2.5 cm) balls. Place, about 2 inches (5 cm) apart, on cookie sheet. Dip the tines of a fork in flour and press dough flat, making a crisscross pattern on top. Bake in preheated oven for 12 to 14 minutes or until dark brown around the edges. Let cool on pan on a rack for 8 to 10 minutes or until firm. Serve warm or transfer to rack and let cool completely.

> ## Variation
>
> Melt ¾ cup (175 mL) vegan chocolate chips and dip half of each cooled cookie into the melted chocolate. Let cool on a wire rack until chocolate is set.

Cranberry Nut Bread (page 170)

Tip

A serrated knife can saw
through the nuts in biscotti
more successfully than
other kinds of knives. This
helps prevent unevenly
shaped biscotti.

Pistachio Lemon Biscotti

❧ *Preheat oven to 325°F (160°C)*
❧ *Large rimless cookie sheet, lined with foil*

2 cups + 2 tbsp	all-purpose flour	525 mL
1½ tsp	baking powder	7 mL
¼ tsp	salt	1 mL
¾ cup	granulated natural cane sugar	175 mL
½ cup	soy margarine	125 mL
	Egg replacer for 2 eggs, prepared according to package directions	
1 tsp	finely grated lemon zest	5 mL
2 tbsp	freshly squeezed lemon juice	25 mL
½ cup	shelled unsalted pistachios	125 mL

1. In a bowl, combine flour, baking powder and salt.

2. In a separate bowl, using an electric mixer, beat sugar
   with margarine on medium speed for 2 minutes or until
   light and fluffy. Beat in egg replacer and lemon zest and
   juice until thoroughly combined. Gradually add flour
   mixture, beating on low speed just until a dough forms.
   Do not overbeat. Mix in pistachios.

3. Divide dough into quarters. On prepared baking sheet,
   shape each portion into a long rectangular log about
   14 inches long by 1½ inches wide by ½ inch thick
   (35 cm long by 4 cm wide by 1 cm thick).

4. Bake in preheated oven for 25 to 30 minutes or until lightly golden and firm. Let cool on pan on a rack for 5 minutes. Transfer to a cutting board. Using a serrated knife, cut each log on a 45-degree angle into $\frac{1}{2}$-inch (1 cm) thick slices. Arrange, cut side up, on baking sheet and bake for 7 minutes longer. Turn slices over and bake for 5 to 8 minutes longer or until dry and toasted. Slide foil with biscotti onto a rack and let cool to room temperature. Store in an airtight container at room temperature for up to 2 weeks or freeze for up to 2 months.

Variations

This is a recipe that can be changed to suit your tastes. If you prefer, use hazelnuts, almonds, walnuts or pine nuts in place of the pistachios.

Add $\frac{1}{3}$ cup (75 mL) dried fruit, such as chopped apricots, cranberries or cherries along with the pistachios. However, we recommend steeping dried fruit in hot water or juice for 1 minute to soften it before you add it to the dough. Otherwise it might get too hard when baked.

Oatmeal Raisin Cookies

These are a quick version of the classic cookie and are a healthy snack for the whole family. Beth's kids — Oriane, Tati and Val — enjoy sneaking raw dough (which in this case is acceptable because there are no raw eggs to worry about) before they even reach cookie form.

❧ Preheat oven to 325°F (160°C)
❧ Large rimless cookie sheets, lined with foil and greased

1¾ cups	all-purpose flour	425 mL
1 tsp	baking soda	5 mL
½ tsp	salt	2 mL
1 cup	packed light brown sugar	250 mL
½ cup	soy margarine	125 mL
3 tbsp	puréed silken tofu	45 mL
½ cup	vegetable oil	125 mL
1 tsp	vanilla	5 mL
1 cup	rolled oats (quick-cooking or old-fashioned)	250 mL
½ cup	raisins	125 mL

1. In a small bowl, combine flour, baking soda and salt.

2. In a separate bowl, using an electric mixer, beat sugar with margarine on medium speed for 2 minutes or until light and fluffy. Add tofu and mix until blended. Add vegetable oil and vanilla and mix well. Gradually add flour mixture, beating on low speed just until a dough forms. Stir in oatmeal and raisins.

3. Drop dough by tablespoonfuls (15 mL), about 2 inches (5 cm) apart, onto prepared baking sheet. Bake in preheated oven for 12 to 15 minutes or until firm and set. Let cool to room temperature on pan on a rack. Store at room temperature in an airtight container for up to 1 week.

Variations

If you're a cinnamon lover, add ¾ tsp (4 mL) ground cinnamon along with the dry ingredients.

Substitute an equal amount of another dried fruit, such as cranberries, currants or chopped dates for the raisins.

Chocolate lovers can add up to ½ cup (125 mL) vegan chocolate chips along with the oats and raisins.

For a refreshing, lemony treat, serve these bars with a fresh fruit salad or sorbet.

Tip

For the best texture, these bars are best eaten within 3 days. Store them in a cookie tin or another airtight container at room temperature.

Lemon Shortbread Bars

❧ *Preheat oven to 325°F (160°C)*
❧ *13-by 9-inch (3 L) baking pan, ungreased*

2½ cups	all-purpose flour	625 mL
1 cup	granulated natural cane sugar	250 mL
1 cup	cold soy margarine	250 mL
2 tsp	finely grated lemon zest	10 mL
3 tbsp	freshly squeezed lemon juice	25 mL
1 to 2 tsp	water, optional	5 to 10 mL
2 tbsp	confectioner's (icing) sugar, sifted	15 mL

1. In a large bowl, combine flour with sugar. Using two knives, a pastry blender or your fingers, cut in margarine until mixture resembles coarse crumbs. Add lemon zest and juice. Stir with a fork until dough comes together. If dough doesn't hold together, gradually add just enough water to make a dry dough.

2. Shape dough into a ball and press evenly into pan. Bake in preheated oven for 40 to 45 minutes or until a tester inserted in the center comes out clean. Remove from oven and immediately dust evenly with confectioner's sugar. Let cool in pan on a rack for 15 minutes. Cut into 2-inch by 1-inch (5 cm by 2.5 cm) bars.

Sticky Pecan Squares

These delicious squares combine the best of two classics: shortbread and pecan pie.

Tips

Although any kind of maple syrup works well in this recipe, using dark, rich Grade B or dark amber maple syrup adds extra depth and character to the caramelized pecans.

Don't worry if the dough doesn't stick together when you are mixing it. It will meld as it bakes.

Use a serrated knife dipped into water to cut neat squares.

🍂 Preheat oven to 350°F (180°C)
🍂 8-inch (2 L) square cake pan, greased

CRUST

1 cup	all-purpose flour	250 mL
½ cup	confectioner's (icing) sugar, sifted	125 mL
½ cup	soy margarine	125 mL

TOPPING

⅓ cup	soy margarine	75 mL
½ cup	packed light brown sugar	125 mL
1½ tbsp	soy creamer	22 mL
¼ cup	pure maple syrup (see Tips, left)	50 mL
Pinch	salt	Pinch
1⅓ cups	coarsely chopped pecans	325 mL

1. *Crust:* In a bowl, mix flour with sugar. Using two forks, a pastry blender or your fingers, cut in margarine until mixture resembles coarse crumbs. Press evenly into prepared pan. Bake in preheated oven for 20 minutes or until light golden and firm.

2. *Topping:* Meanwhile, in a pot, melt margarine over medium heat. Add brown sugar and soy creamer and cook, stirring, for 1 minute or until blended and heated through. Reduce heat to low. Add maple syrup and salt and cook, stirring, for 1 minute. Add pecans, stirring until evenly coated.

3. Spread pecan mixture evenly over hot crust. Bake for 20 to 23 minutes longer or until topping is set and pecans are fragrant. Let cool to room temperature in pan on a rack. Cut into squares.

Variations

Chocolate lovers can add a drizzle of melted chocolate to these bars. After the bars have cooled to room temperature, melt ¼ cup (50 mL) vegan chocolate chips with 2 tsp (10 mL) vegetable oil. Dip the tines of a fork into the mixture and drizzle threads of melted chocolate over the pecans.

Replace pecan pieces with walnut pieces to make Sticky Walnut Squares.

Brownies

Tip

The regular skewer test for doneness doesn't work well on this recipe because the batter contains chocolate chips. If you test through a melted chip, the tester won't come out clean.

❧Preheat oven to 350°F (180°C)
❧13-by 9-inch (3 L) baking pan, greased

1 ½ cups	vegan chocolate chips, divided	375 mL
¾ cup	soy margarine	175 mL
1 ½ cups	all-purpose flour	375 mL
½ cup	unsweetened cocoa powder	125 mL
½ tsp	baking powder	2 mL
9 oz	silken tofu (extra-firm or firm)	275 g
1 ½ cups	granulated natural cane sugar	375 mL
1 tsp	vanilla	5 mL
½ cup	corn syrup (dark or light)	125 mL

1. In a small heavy pot, combine 1 cup (250 mL) chocolate chips with margarine. Melt over low heat, stirring until smooth. Remove from heat and set aside.

2. In a bowl, sift together flour, cocoa powder and baking powder. Set aside.

3. Holding the tofu over a bowl or sink, gently squeeze to release excess liquid. Transfer to a blender. Add sugar and vanilla and blend until smooth.

4. In a large bowl, combine melted chocolate with corn syrup. Add tofu mixture and mix well. Fold in flour mixture just until moistened. Add remaining ½ cup (125 mL) chocolate chips and fold until evenly distributed through batter.

5. Spread batter in prepared pan, smoothing the top and pushing batter into the corners. Bake in preheated oven for 25 to 35 minutes or until center is firm. Let cool completely in pan on a wire rack. Cut into squares.

Variation

Add ½ cup (125 mL) dried fruits, nuts or peanut butter chips along with the chocolate chips. Dried sour cherries produce a variation that is reminiscent of a Black Forest torte.

Apple Muffins

With the help of Beth's friend, Louise, who is a vegan pastry chef, Beth developed this basic muffin recipe. It calls for easy-to-find ingredients, but the recipe is flexible enough to allow for customization, using your favorite spices, fruits and nuts.

Tips

Apples that have a soft texture when cooked, such as McIntosh and Cortland, are preferred in this recipe because they add moisture.

Substitute plain rice milk or almond milk plus 1 tsp (5 mL) vanilla for the vanilla-flavor soy milk.

Transfer cooled muffins to a resealable plastic bag or airtight container and freeze for up to 6 weeks.

❧ Preheat oven to 375°F (190°C)
❧ 12-cup muffin tin, lined with paper liners or greased

2 cups	all-purpose flour	500 mL
1 1/2 tbsp	baking powder	22 mL
2 tsp	pumpkin pie spice (or 1 tsp/5 mL ground cinnamon and 1/2 tsp/2 mL ground nutmeg)	10 mL
3/4 tsp	salt	4 mL
3/4 cup	vanilla-flavor soy milk (see Tips, left)	175 mL
1/2 cup	pure maple syrup	125 mL
1/4 cup	vegetable or olive oil	50 mL
1/4 cup	unsweetened apple juice	50 mL
1 1/2 cups	diced cored (unpeeled) apples	375 mL
1/2 cup	raisins	125 mL
1/2 cup	walnut pieces	125 mL
	Granulated natural cane sugar or other dry sweetener	

1. In a large bowl, mix together flour, baking powder, pumpkin pie spice and salt.

2. In a separate bowl, whisk together soy milk, maple syrup, oil and apple juice.

3. Using a wooden spoon, make a well in the middle of the flour mixture. Pour soy milk mixture into the well and stir just until the dry ingredients are moistened. Fold in apples, raisins and walnuts. Spoon batter evenly into prepared muffin pan. Sprinkle a pinch of sugar on top of each muffin.

4. Bake in preheated oven for 22 to 25 minutes or until tops are firm to the touch. Let cool in pan on a rack for 10 minutes. Remove from pan and serve or let cool completely.

Variations

Add your favorite spices to the batter. For instance, 1/2 tsp (2 mL) ground ginger can be added alone or along with 1/4 tsp (1 mL) ground cloves or 1/4 tsp (1 mL) ground allspice.

Replace apples with 1 1/2 cups (375 mL) coarsely chopped or mashed bananas (about 2) and substitute 3/4 cup (175 mL) vegan chocolate chips for the walnuts.

For perfect little grab-and-go snacks, bake this recipe in mini-muffin tins. Decrease baking time to about 13 minutes.

Banana Chocolate Chip Pudding Bread

Rich and gooey, this is not a typical bread — hence the name "pudding bread." More of a dessert than a breakfast bread, this dense, filling loaf is easy to prepare and great for company.

Tips

Usually all-purpose flour does not need to be sifted, but because there are no eggs in this batter, it is quite thick. We feel that sifting adds airiness, which is necessary to lighten the result.

Silken tofu can be lumpy when mixed with other ingredients. Mashing it before blending and mixing it with the banana before adding the other ingredients helps to eliminate this problem.

Because this bread is so moist, a toothpick inserted in the center will not come out clean even when it is cooked. As a result, we use an alternative test for doneness.

➣ *Preheat oven to 350°F (180°C)*
➣ *9-by 5-inch (1.5 L) loaf pan, greased and floured*

2½ cups	all-purpose flour	625 mL
1 tbsp	baking powder	15 mL
½ tsp	salt	2 mL
1½ cups	mashed ripe bananas (3 to 4 medium)	375 mL
¼ cup	mashed soft silken tofu (see Tips, left)	50 mL
1¼ cups	vanilla-flavor soy milk	300 mL
¾ cup	granulated natural cane sugar	175 mL
¼ cup	vegetable oil	50 mL
¾ cup	vegan chocolate chips	175 mL

1. In a large bowl, sift together flour, baking powder and salt.

2. In a separate bowl, using a fork, mix bananas and tofu until blended. Add soy milk, sugar and oil and mix well. Stir in chocolate chips. Add to flour mixture and stir well.

3. Spread in prepared pan, smoothing top. Bake for 1 hour and 10 minutes or until firm in the middle when pressed with the back of a spoon. If the depression from the spoon remains, the center is not yet set. Bake for another 3 to 5 minutes or until the middle is firm. Let cool in pan on a rack for 20 minutes, then transfer to rack and let cool completely.

Variation

Add ½ cup (125 mL) chopped walnuts along with the chocolate chips.

Cranberry Nut Bread

This bread is just the thing for entertaining in the afternoon with coffee or tea, or for dessert after a light lunch. It also makes a nice holiday gift. It freezes very well — just wrap the loaf tightly in plastic wrap.

Tips

In this recipe, we sift the flour to aerate the batter.

Using melted margarine, rather than oil, adds a richer color to the bread.

In place of vanilla-flavor rice milk or soy milk, substitute a plain version and add 1 tsp (5 mL) vanilla.

❧ Preheat oven to 350°F (180°C)
❧ 9-by 5-inch (1.5 L) loaf pan, greased and floured

2½ cups	all-purpose flour	625 mL
1 tbsp	baking powder	15 mL
½ tsp	salt	2 mL
	Egg replacer for 1 egg, prepared according to package directions	
¾ cup	granulated natural cane sugar or other dry sweetener	175 mL
¼ cup	melted soy margarine or vegetable oil	50 mL
1 tsp	finely grated orange zest	5 mL
1¼ cups	vanilla-flavor rice milk or soy milk	300 mL
½ cup	chopped pecans	125 mL
½ cup	dried cranberries	125 mL

1. In a large bowl, sift together flour, baking powder and salt.

2. In a separate bowl, whisk together egg replacer, sugar, margarine and orange zest. Add rice milk and mix well. Add liquid mixture to flour mixture and stir vigorously for 1 minute or until smooth. Stir in pecans and dried cranberries.

3. Scrape batter into prepared pan, smoothing top. Bake in preheated oven for 50 to 55 minutes or until a tester inserted in the center comes out clean. Let cool in pan on a rack for 20 minutes. Transfer to rack and let cool completely.

Variations

If you like tangy flavors, replace the dried cranberries with ¾ cup (175 mL) coarsely chopped fresh cranberries.

Substitute chopped walnuts for the pecans.

Cranberry Orange Scones

Tips

Many margarines contain salt, so we have not added salt in this recipe. If you are using unsalted margarine, add ½ tsp (2 mL) salt along with the baking powder.

These scones freeze well. Let them cool to room temperature, then transfer to resealable plastic freezer bags or an airtight container and freeze for up to 6 weeks. Reheat directly from freezer in a 350°F (180°C) oven for 10 to 12 minutes or until heated through.

Substitute an equal amount of diced dried apricots or raisins for the cranberries. You can also substitute walnuts for the pecans.

❧ *Preheat oven to 400°F (200°C)*
❧ *Large rimless baking sheet, greased*

6 tbsp	freshly squeezed orange juice	90 mL
⅓ cup	dried cranberries (see Tips, left)	75 mL
2 cups	all-purpose flour	500 mL
⅓ cup	granulated natural cane sugar	75 mL
2 tsp	baking powder	10 mL
½ cup	cold soy margarine (see Tips, left)	125 mL
	Egg replacer for 2 eggs, prepared according to package directions	
1 tsp	finely grated orange zest	5 mL
1 tsp	vanilla	5 mL
½ cup	pecans, coarsely chopped, optional	125 mL
	Granulated natural cane sugar, optional	

1. In a small saucepan over medium heat, bring orange juice and dried cranberries to a simmer. Simmer for 3 minutes or until cranberries are softened. Let cool to room temperature. Strain cranberries, reserving liquid. Set cranberries and liquid aside.

2. In a bowl, mix together flour, sugar and baking powder. Using two forks, a pastry blender or your fingers, cut in margarine until mixture forms pea-size crumbs.

3. In a small bowl, combine egg replacer, orange zest and vanilla. Add reserved cranberry liquid and mix well. Add to flour mixture and stir with a wooden spoon or use your fingers to mix the dough until it holds together, taking care not to overmix. (It may feel crumbly.) With lightly floured hands, lightly knead in cranberries and pecans, if using, just until evenly distributed through dough.

4. Keeping hands floured, place dough on prepared baking sheet and shape into a 9-inch (23 cm) round disc. Using a serrated knife, cut into eight wedges, leaving them intact. Sprinkle sugar over top, if using. Bake in preheated oven for 20 to 25 minutes or until golden. Let cool on pan on a rack for 5 minutes before serving.

Hot Chocolate Baguette

🍥 *Preheat oven to 375°F (190°C)*

| 1 | French baguette (about 16 inches/40 cm long) | 1 |
| 2/3 cup | vegan chocolate chips or chopped semisweet chocolate | 150 mL |

1. Cut baguette in half lengthwise, not cutting all the way through so that the bread opens up like a book. Sprinkle chocolate evenly in a strip down the opening.

2. Wrap loaf in a large piece of aluminum foil. Bake in preheated oven for 20 to 25 minutes or until the smell of chocolate and freshly baked bread begins to permeate the kitchen.

3. Let cool in foil for 3 to 5 minutes. Unwrap and cut into thick slices. Serve immediately.

Phyllo Cups

❧ *Preheat oven to 375°F (190°C)*
❧ *12-cup muffin tin, greased*

| 5 or 10 | sheets phyllo pastry, thawed (see Tips, left) | 5 or 10 |
| 2/3 cup | soy margarine or buttery spread, melted | 150 mL |

1. Stack phyllo sheets with edges aligned. Depending on size of sheets (see Tips, left) cut through all the layers of phyllo to make six or twelve 4$\frac{1}{2}$-inch (11.25 cm) squares. (You will have 60 squares in total.) Cover with a moist towel to prevent phyllo from drying out.

2. Brush one square of phyllo lightly with margarine. Brush a second square with margarine and place on top of the first at a slight angle. Continue brushing and layering in this manner, working with one square at a time, adding three more squares to make five layers total. (The five layers stacked together should look like a star with multiple points.) Using your fingers, press stack into a prepared muffin cup, pressing center against bottom of the cup and letting the sides fold and ripple like cloth. Repeat with remaining phyllo squares and margarine.

3. Bake in preheated oven for 8 to 10 minutes or until golden brown. Let cool in pan on a rack for 2 to 3 minutes. Transfer to rack and let cool completely or fill and serve immediately.

These phyllo cups combine the best of both worlds: they look fancy but are simple to make and they add a note of elegance to any table. They make wonderful dessert containers (see Variations, below) but they also work well for savory dishes (see Roasted Vegetables in Phyllo Cups, page 157).

Tips

Most 1-lb (500 g) packages of phyllo contain two 8-oz (250 g) rolls. The sheets are approximately 18 by 14 inches (45 by 35 cm) or 9 by 14 inches (22.5 by 35 cm). For this recipe, we use half of one roll. Depending upon the dimensions, you will use five or 10 sheets. The remaining phyllo can be refrozen once, after which it becomes quite brittle. Roll tightly and seal well with plastic wrap.

To add taste and texture, sprinkle finely ground walnuts or almonds, a pinch of sugar and cinnamon, nutmeg or allspice between layers.

Use a serrated knife for best results when cutting phyllo.

Fill these cups on the plate on which they are to be served. A flat utensil works best for serving.

These cups freeze well. After cooling to room temperature, freeze in an airtight container for up to 1 month.

Variations

Fruit-Filled Phyllo Cups: In a large bowl, combine 4 cups (1 L) mixed soft fruit, such as berries, grapes, sliced halved bananas, sliced quartered kiwifruit or cubed mango, papaya and/or melon ($\frac{1}{2}$-inch/1 cm cubes). Toss with $\frac{1}{4}$ cup (50 mL) maple syrup. Fill each cup with about $\frac{1}{3}$ cup (75 mL) of the mixture.

Chocolate Pudding–Filled Phyllo Cups: Fill each phyllo cup with $\frac{1}{3}$ cup (75 mL) Chocolate Pudding (see recipe, page 120), then top with 1 tbsp (15 mL) berries or banana slices.

Apple and Soy Yogurt–Filled Phyllo Cups: Fill each phyllo cup with vanilla–flavor soy yogurt and top with a dollop of Luscious Apple Butter (see recipe, page 105).

Sorbet–Filled Phyllo Cups with Fresh Berries: Fill each phyllo cup with a scoop of your favorite fruit sorbet and garnish with 2 tbsp (25 mL) fresh berries.

Pie Crust

We developed this pastry so you can press it into a pie dish without using a rolling pin. This technique results in a flaky, tender crust. Not only is it simple, but it is also a great time-saver. Use it with your favorite filling or when making Fudge Pie (see recipe, page 176) or Pumpkin Pie (see recipe, page 175).

Tips

Soy spreads have more moisture than margarine, and some contain more salt. If you are concerned about salt in your diet, omit the salt in this recipe.

Weighting the pie shell with beans or weights helps it hold its shape and prevents bubbles or distortions from forming as it bakes.

❧ Preheat oven to 425°F (220°C)
❧ 9-inch (23 cm) pie plate, greased

1 ½ cups	all-purpose flour	375 mL
½ tsp	salt	2 mL
½ cup	soy margarine (see Tips, left)	125 mL
2 to 3 tbsp	cold soy creamer or other dairy-free beverage	25 to 45 mL

1. In a bowl, combine flour with salt. Using two knives, a pastry blender or your fingers, cut in margarine until mixture resembles coarse crumbs. Drizzle with soy creamer, 1 tbsp (15 mL) at a time, pressing the dough with your fingers as it starts to moisten. When it begins to hold together in large clumps, you have added enough soy creamer.

2. Place dough on a flat, lightly floured surface. Use the palm of one hand to push down on dough and drag it forward 6 to 8 inches (15 to 20 cm). Repeat this motion three or four times until you have worked all of the dough into a soft, pliable texture. Gather dough together and press into a disc.

3. With floured fingers or the back of a spoon, press dough into pie plate, pressing and pushing out toward the side and up toward the rim. Flute or crimp edge with the tines of a fork.

4. Cover with plastic wrap and refrigerate for at least 30 minutes or for up to 24 hours.

5. Line dough with foil and fill with 2 cups (500 mL) dried beans or pie weights (see Tips, left). Bake on bottom rack of preheated oven for 10 to 15 minutes or until set. Remove beans and foil. Reduce temperature to 350°F (180°C). Bake for 10 minutes longer or until crust is light golden. Let cool to room temperature on a rack before filling.

Pumpkin Pie

This pumpkin pie, made without eggs and milk, has all the texture and taste of the traditional version.

Tips

Make sure to buy pumpkin purée, not pumpkin pie filling, which is seasoned.

If you prefer, use a combination of 1 tsp (5 mL) ground cinnamon and ½ tsp (2 mL) ground ginger instead of the pumpkin pie spice.

Use a prepared pie shell or make your own (see recipe, page 174).

This pie should be refrigerated after cooling. It will keep for up to 4 days. Do not freeze, because freezing causes the crust to separate from the filling.

🌿 Preheat oven to 425°F (220°C)
🌿 Food processor

1 cup	pitted dates (18 to 20), halved	250 mL
¾ cup	water	175 mL
6 oz	firm silken tofu	175 g
1	can (14 or 15 oz/398 or 426 mL) pumpkin purée (see Tips, left)	1
½ cup	pure maple syrup	125 mL
1½ tsp	pumpkin pie spice (see Tips, left)	7 mL
½ tsp	salt	2 mL
1 tbsp	dry egg replacer powder	15 mL
1 tsp	vanilla	5 mL
1	9-inch (23 cm) vegan pie shell, unbaked (see Tips, left)	1

1. In a small saucepan, combine dates with water. Bring to a boil over high heat and cook for 3 minutes or until very soft. (Dates should offer no resistance when pressed with a wooden spoon.) Remove from heat and drain, reserving liquid. Set dates aside.

2. In food processor, process tofu until smooth, scraping down the side of the bowl. Add reserved dates and all but ⅓ cup (75 mL) of the cooking liquid from the dates, setting the remainder aside. Process until smooth. Add pumpkin purée, maple syrup, pumpkin pie spice and salt. Process until smooth.

3. With motor running, add egg replacer powder through the feed tube. Add remaining date cooking liquid and vanilla and process until blended.

4. Pour filling into pie shell, smoothing surface with a spoon or spatula. Bake in preheated oven for 20 minutes. Reduce oven temperature to 350°F (180°C) and bake for 30 to 35 minutes longer or until crust is lightly browned and filling is dark, firm in the center and fragrant. Let cool completely on a rack.

Variations

Before baking, arrange ⅔ cup (150 mL) pecan halves around the rim of the filling, pressing lightly into the surface.

When serving, drizzle each piece with soy creamer and top with flecks of finely chopped crystallized ginger.

Make this recipe and you will understand where the expression "easy as pie" comes from. Even better, it's decadent. Serve with a scoop of fruit sorbet to contrast the deep chocolate essence.

Tips

Use a prepared crust or make your own (see recipe, page 174).

Vegan chocolate chips are dark chocolate chips made without any milk or milk products. You can find them in the natural foods section of most grocery stores. The label will say that they are dairy-free.

Fudge Pie

Preheat oven to 400°F (200°C)

1	9-inch (23 cm) vegan pie shell, unbaked (see Tips, left)	1
1 cup	light corn syrup	250 mL
½ cup	soy margarine	125 mL
¾ cup	vegan chocolate chips	175 mL
½ cup	unsweetened cocoa powder, sifted	125 mL
1 tsp	vanilla	5 mL

1. Using a fork, gently prick bottom and sides of pie shell. Bake in preheated oven for 15 minutes or until brown around edges. Let cool to room temperature.

2. Meanwhile, in a saucepan over medium-low heat, melt corn syrup with margarine. Pour into a bowl and add chocolate chips, whisking until melted. Add cocoa powder and vanilla and mix well. Pour into pie shell. Refrigerate for 2 to 3 hours or until chilled and set.

Variation

Serve with sliced fresh strawberries or whole raspberries for an added treat.

This crisp is a family pleaser year-round. We like to make it using light brown muscovado sugar, an unrefined sugar that retains its rich molasses and caramel flavor. It goes particularly well with the tart flavors of Granny Smith apples and lemon.

Tips

If you don't have muscovado sugar on hand, you can use an equal amount of brown sugar, sucanat or even granulated natural cane sugar.

Use your favorite variety of apple. McIntosh apples have excellent flavor but don't hold their shape as well as Golden Delicious or Granny Smith in baking and tend to produce a texture that is more like applesauce.

Apple Crisp

Preheat oven to 375°F (190°C)
8-inch (2 L) square baking dish, greased

6	Granny Smith apples (or other tart cooking apples), peeled, cored and thinly sliced	6
1 cup	light brown muscovado sugar or other dry sweetener, divided	250 mL
½ tsp	finely grated lemon zest	2 mL
1½ tbsp	freshly squeezed lemon juice, divided (see Tips, left)	22 mL
1 cup	all-purpose flour	250 mL
½ cup	rolled oats (old-fashioned or quick-cooking)	125 mL
½ tsp	ground cinnamon	2 mL
½ tsp	ground nutmeg	2 mL
½ cup	soy margarine	125 mL
½ cup	almonds, coarsely chopped	125 mL

1. In a bowl, combine apples, ½ cup (125 mL) sugar and lemon zest and juice. Toss until evenly coated. Spread evenly in prepared baking dish.

2. In a separate bowl, combine flour, rolled oats, remaining ½ cup (125 mL) sugar, cinnamon and nutmeg. Using two knives, a pastry blender or your fingers, cut in margarine until mixture resembles coarse crumbs. Mix in almonds. Sprinkle evenly over apples.

3. Bake in preheated oven for 50 to 55 minutes or until the topping is browned, juices are bubbling and apples are soft when pierced with a fork. Serve hot or at room temperature.

Variations

This recipe can be made with other fruits instead of apples. We also like to use sour cherries, blueberries (substitute lime zest and juice for the lemon) or a combination of equal parts strawberries and rhubarb.

Substitute pecans or walnuts for the almonds, if you prefer.

Indian Pudding

This dessert is a classic. When Beth worked at the Harvard Faculty Club in Cambridge, Massachusetts, it was a perennial favorite, so she made it daily. We think this vegan version is every bit as good as the original.

Tip

Because cornmeal lumps easily when added directly to hot liquids, we prefer to whisk it first with cold water.

➤ *Preheat oven to 375°F (190°C)*
➤ *12-cup (3 L) ovenproof pot, or casserole dish, greased*

4 cups	soy creamer	1 L
1 tsp	vanilla	5 mL
¼ tsp	ground cinnamon	1 mL
Pinch	salt	Pinch
2½ cups	cold water	625 mL
¾ cup	cornmeal	175 mL
1 cup	fancy molasses	250 mL
⅓ cup	golden or dark raisins	75 mL

1. In a pot over high heat, bring soy creamer to a simmer. Add vanilla, cinnamon and salt. Remove from heat.

2. Meanwhile, in a bowl, whisk cold water with cornmeal. Add to soy creamer mixture, a little at a time, whisking constantly, to prevent lumps from forming. Whisk in molasses and mix thoroughly. Stir in raisins.

3. Return pot to medium–high heat and cook, whisking constantly, until pudding begins to bubble. If pot is not ovenproof, transfer pudding to prepared casserole dish.

4. Bake in preheated oven, stirring halfway though and scraping down sides of dish, for 50 minutes or until pudding mounds on a spoon. Let cool for 5 minutes. Serve hot.

Variation

This pudding pairs well with fresh fruit, such as blueberries or sautéed apple slices. We also enjoy it with vanilla-flavor soy yogurt and a dollop of Luscious Apple Butter (see recipe, page 105).

Rice Pudding with Raisins

Tip

If you prefer your pudding with a thicker consistency, serve it cold. As the pudding cools, it firms up.

4 cups	vanilla-flavor rice milk or soy milk	1 L
1 cup	short-grain rice	250 mL
$\frac{1}{3}$ cup	granulated natural cane sugar or other dry sweetener	75 mL
$\frac{1}{2}$ tsp	ground cinnamon	2 mL
$\frac{1}{4}$ tsp	salt	1 mL
$\frac{3}{4}$ cup	dark raisins	175 mL
2 tbsp	orange juice or dark rum	25 mL
	Ground cinnamon, optional	

1. In a large heavy pot, combine rice milk, rice, sugar, cinnamon and salt. Bring to a boil over medium heat, stirring constantly, until sugar is dissolved. Reduce heat to low and simmer, stirring occasionally, for 20 minutes or until rice is tender and mixture is creamy. Taste a spoonful to ensure the rice is thoroughly cooked. If not, continue cooking for a few more minutes.

2. In a small pot, over medium–high heat, combine raisins with orange juice. Cook, stirring, for 1 minute or until raisins are plump and orange juice is absorbed. Add to cooked pudding and mix thoroughly. Serve hot, or chill for at least 2 hours and serve cold.

Variations

Add $\frac{1}{4}$ tsp (1 mL) ground cardamom along with the cinnamon.

Cook 2 tbsp (25 mL) finely chopped candied ginger along with the raisins.

Pour 1 cup (250 mL) soy creamer over the cooked pudding to enhance its texture and taste.

Summer Fruit Compote

Tips

To get extra duty from
vanilla beans, lightly rinse
and air-dry them, then add
the split pieces to a jar of
sugar to make vanilla sugar.
The split bean can stay
indefinitely in the sugar
jar, as you use and
replenish your supply.

Use a variety of fruits to
make up the total volume
of 8 cups (2 L). Add the
firmest fruit, such as
apples, peaches and pears,
to the hot syrup first, then
continue in order of the
fruit's texture, ending with
the most fragile fruits, such
as raspberries or pieces
of melon. Mix carefully
so that the tender fruit
doesn't break or bruise.

3½ cups	water	875 mL
1 cup	granulated natural cane sugar or other dry sweetener	250 mL
1	vanilla bean, split lengthwise (or 2 tsp /10 mL vanilla extract)	1
4	strips (2 inches by ½ inch/5 by 1 cm) lime zest	4
2 cups	diced peeled pitted peaches, nectarines or apricots	500 mL
1 cup	diced pitted plums (about 2)	250 mL
1 cup	fresh cherries, pitted and halved	250 mL
2 cups	fresh berries (see Tips, left)	500 mL
2 cups	cantaloupe or honeydew melon balls (1 inch /2.5 cm)	500 mL
⅓ cup	freshly squeezed lime juice (about 3 limes)	75 mL

1. In a large pot, bring water and sugar to a boil over high heat, stirring until sugar is dissolved. Add vanilla bean and lime zest. Remove from heat, cover and let stand for 6 to 8 minutes or until fragrant.

2. Add peaches, plums, cherries, berries, then melon to syrup and stir to combine. Add lime juice and mix well. Let stand at room temperature for at least 3 hours to develop full flavor. Transfer to an airtight container and refrigerate for up to 3 days. Remove vanilla bean and lime zest before serving.

Variations

Use lemons or oranges instead of limes.

For a more sophisticated version, add ¼ cup (50 mL) dark rum or orange-flavored brandy along with the lime juice.

Library and Archives Canada Cataloguing in Publication

Chuck, Maxine Effenson
   125 best vegan recipes / Maxine Effenson Chuck & Beth Gurney.

Includes index.
ISBN 0-7788-0113-6

1. Vegan cookery. I. Gurney, Beth II. Title. III. Title: One hundred twenty-five
best vegan recipes.

TX837.C585 2005   641.5'636   C2004-906536-X

Resources

Informative Reading

Kilham, Christopher S. *The Bread & Circus Whole Food Bible* (Reading, MA: Addison-Wesley Publishing Co., Inc., 1991).

Lappé, Frances Moore. *Diet for a Small Planet* (New York: Ballantine Books, 1982).

Marcus, Erik. *Vegan: The New Ethics of Eating* (Ithaca, NY: McBooks Press, 2001).

Ornish, Dean, M.D. *Eat More, Weigh Less* (New York: Harper Paperbacks, 1993).

Willett, Walter C., M.D. *Eat, Drink and Be Healthy* (New York: Simon & Schuster, 2001).

Vegan-friendly food suppliers

www.naturesflavors.com
www.goodnessdirect.co.uk
www.kingarthurflour.com
www.penzeys.com
www.wildoats.com

For information about the vegan lifestyle

www.veganoutreach.org
www.veganessentials.com
www.andrews.edu/NUFS/Children.html
www.knowledgehound.com/topics/vegetarr.htm#vegan
www.vegan.org.nz

Index

More Great Books from Robert Rose

Appliance Cooking

- 125 Best Microwave Oven Recipes
  by Johanna Burkhard
- The Blender Bible
  by Andrew Chase and Nicole Young
- 125 Best Pressure Cooker Recipes
  by Cinda Chavich
- The 150 Best Slow Cooker Recipes
  by Judith Finlayson
- Delicious & Dependable Slow Cooker Recipes
  by Judith Finlayson
- 125 Best Vegetarian Slow Cooker Recipes
  by Judith Finlayson
- 125 Best Rotisserie Oven Recipes
  by Judith Finlayson
- The Best Family Slow Cooker Recipes
  by Donna-Marie Pye
- 125 Best Indoor Grill Recipes
  by Ilana Simon
- The Best Convection Oven Cookbook
  by Linda Stephen
- 125 Best Toaster Oven Recipes
  by Linda Stephen
- 250 Best American Bread Machine Baking Recipes
  by Donna Washburn and Heather Butt
- 250 Best Canadian Bread Machine Baking Recipes
  by Donna Washburn and Heather Butt

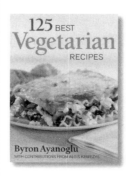

Baking

- 250 Best Cakes & Pies
  by Esther Brody
- 250 Best Cobblers, Custards, Cupcakes, Bread Puddings & More
  by Esther Brody
- 500 Best Cookies, Bars & Squares
  by Esther Brody
- 500 Best Muffin Recipes
  by Esther Brody
- 125 Best Cheesecake Recipes
  by George Geary
- 125 Best Chocolate Recipes
  by Julie Hasson
- 125 Best Chocolate Chip Recipes
  by Julie Hasson
- 125 Best Cupcake Recipes
  by Julie Hasson

Healthy Cooking

- 125 Best Vegetarian Recipes
  by Byron Ayanoglu with contributions from Alexis Kemezys
- America's Best Cookbook for Kids with Diabetes
  by Colleen Bartley
- Canada's Best Cookbook for Kids with Diabetes
  by Colleen Bartley
- The Juicing Bible
  by Pat Crocker and Susan Eagles

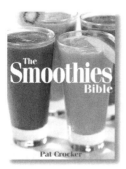

- The Smoothies Bible
  by Pat Crocker
- 125 Best Vegan
  Recipes
  *by Maxine Effenson Chuck
  and Beth Gurney*

- 500 Best Healthy
  Recipes
  Edited by Lynn Roblin, RD
- 125 Best Gluten-Free
  Recipes
  *by Donna Washburn
  and Heather Butt*
- The Best Gluten-Free
  Family Cookbook
  *by Donna Washburn
  and Heather Butt*

- America's Everyday
  Diabetes Cookbook
  *Edited by Katherine
  E. Younker, MBA, RD*
- Canada's Everyday
  Diabetes Choice
  Recipes
  *Edited by Katherine
  E. Younker, MBA, RD*
- Canada's Complete
  Diabetes Cookbook
  *Edited by Katherine
  E. Younker, MBA, RD*
- The Best Diabetes
  Cookbook (U.S.)
  *Edited by Katherine
  E. Younker, MBA, RD*

- The Best Low-carb
  Cookbook
  from Robert Rose

Recent Bestsellers

- The Convenience Cook
  by Judith Finlayson
- 125 Best Ice
  Cream Recipes
  *by Marilyn Linton
  and Tanya Linton*

- Easy Indian Cooking
  by Suneeta Vaswani
- Simply Thai Cooking
  *by Wandee Young
  and Byron Ayanoglu*

Health

- The Complete Natural
  Medicine Guide to the
  50 Most Common
  Medicinal Herbs
  *by Dr. Heather Boon,
  B.Sc.Phm., Ph.D. and
  Michael Smith, B.Pharm,
  M.R.Pharm.S., ND*

- The Complete
  Kid's Allergy and
  Asthma Guide
  Edited by Dr. Milton Gold
- The Complete Natural
  Medicine Guide to
  Breast Cancer
  by Sat Dharam Kaur, ND

- The Complete Doctor's
  Stress Solution
  *by Penny Kendall-Reed,
  MSc, ND and Dr. Stephen
  Reed, MD, FRCSC*
- The Complete Doctor's
  Healthy Back Bible
  *by Dr. Stephen Reed, MD
  and Penny Kendall-Reed,
  MSc, ND with Dr. Michael
  Ford, MD, FRCSC and
  Dr. Charles Gregory,
  MD, ChB, FRCP(C)*

- Everyday Risks
  in Pregnancy
  & Breastfeeding
  *by Dr. Gideon Koren,
  MD, FRCP(C), ND*
- Help for Eating
  Disorders
  *by Dr. Debra Katzman,
  MD, FRCP(C) and Dr.
  Leora Pinhas, MD*

Also Available
from Robert Rose

125 best
**Vegetarian
Slow Cooker**
recipes

Judith Finlayson

For more great books, see previous pages